EARLY AMERICAN WALL PAINTINGS
1710-1850

Library of American Art

EARLY AMERICAN
WALL PAINTINGS
1710-1850

By Edward B. Allen

Kennedy Graphics, Inc. • *Da Capo Press*
New York • 1971

This edition of
Early American Wall Paintings, 1710-1850
is an unabridged republication of the first
edition published in New Haven, Connecticut,
in 1926.

Library of Congress Catalog Card Number 77-77694

SBN 306-71332-2

Published by Da Capo Press
A Division of Plenum Publishing Corporation
227 West 17th Street, New York, N.Y. 10011

EARLY AMERICAN
WALL PAINTINGS

THE BAY OF NAPLES

FRESCO BY CORNÈ IN THE SULLIVAN DORR HOUSE, PROVIDENCE, RHODE ISLAND

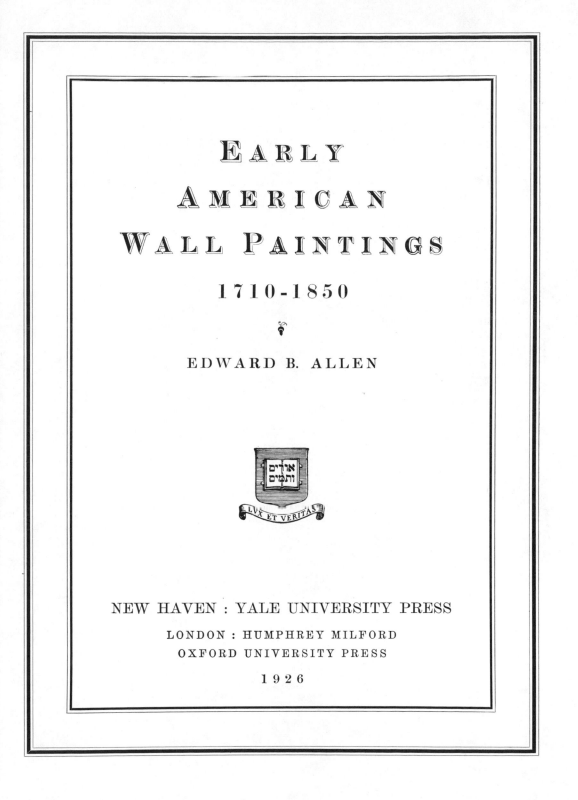

Early
American
Wall Paintings
1710-1850

EDWARD B. ALLEN

NEW HAVEN : YALE UNIVERSITY PRESS

LONDON : HUMPHREY MILFORD
OXFORD UNIVERSITY PRESS

1926

CONTENTS

ILLUSTRATIONS

Photographs indicated by an asterisk (*) are by Charles Darling, Salem, Massachusetts.

FOREWORD

THE first artistic efforts of the white men in America were made by the French explorers. Champlain adorned his journal with pictures in color, and earlier still Jacques le Moyne, the official artist of Ribault's expedition, had depicted the scenes and adventures of that unfortunate colonizing attempt in Florida.

Later came to the English-speaking colonies itinerant portrait painters, who did not disdain the painting of coaches, coats-of-arms, houses, tavern and shop signs, as opportunity offered, and in the opening years of the eighteenth century the first of our historic wall paintings made their appearance in the homes of the colonial aristocracy, the officers of the crown, and wealthy merchants.

These old wall pictures, with the exception of several in Virginia and Yeamans' Hall near Charleston, South Carolina (built prior to 1680 and destroyed by the great earthquake), are strangely enough confined to New England. Probably it was a natural reaction to the early religious prejudice against all forms of art and luxury.

The oldest group of paintings comprises the wainscot panels in the parlors of the Clark house in Boston and "Marmion" in Virginia. They are rich in color, and are adorned with figures, flowers, landscapes, or escutcheons. Included with these is a series of single panels, one to a room. These are for the most part landscapes, and some, in their very crudeness, have the charm of the grotesque.

The frescoes, a much larger group, include scenes by the Italian Cornè; American landscapes in panorama form, by native artists; Masonic and Federal emblems, sailing-ships and steamboats, streets, houses, and people; copies in outline of Flaxman's illustrations of the Iliad; and many excellent stencil and free-hand designs, apparently derived from the peasant art of Europe.

The latest frescoes to be described, on the walls of the Alsop house in Middletown, form a separate group, unrelated to the rest, and are perhaps the work of Brumidi, who painted the frescoes in the Capitol at Washington.

The author's interest in the fascinating subject of early American wall decoration began in boyhood, and he remembers vividly his sensations of wonder and surprise on first entering a room adorned with frescoes. This was in a house in Brattleboro, Vermont. Along with many others worthy of preservation, it has since been destroyed, and no record exists of its painted walls, or of the hand that painted them.

Since that time the author has spent many years searching for the frescoes and panels described in the present volume, and in tracing their history. In making a permanent record of the glories of these old houses, he feels that he has performed a worth-while task; for many of them are fast crumbling to decay, and within a few short years but few will remain.

The author wishes to express his gratitude to the owners of the houses described, and of the panels taken from houses no longer in existence, for their kindness in permitting the photographic reproductions contained in this volume.

E. B. A.

Lynn, Massachusetts,
  July 9, 1926.

THE PICTURE PANELS

CLARK HOUSE
MARMION
SINGLE PANELS

10. SMALL PANEL OVER DOOR FROM "MARMION"

THE PICTURE PANELS

Clark House

THE first period begins with the Clark-Frankland house of Boston, because the pictured wall decorations in its famous parlor (about 1712-1714) were probably the first in New England.

That section of Boston known as the Old North End—now a tenement district in whose narrow streets a strange medley of foreign tongues makes a babel of voices, where on saints' days and *fiestas* picturesque and colorful throngs crowd the hucksters and the sidewalk vendors—this squalid quarter was once the exclusive and aristocratic section of the city.

Quaint as were the gabled buildings with their overhanging stories and latticed windows, the names of the streets were no less curious: Sun Court, Scarlet's Wharf Lane, Ship Street, Salutation Alley, White Bread Alley, Bell Alley, and Garden Court Street. Enlivening the business section were queer, toylike signs in front of shops and taverns, representing naval officers with sextant or spyglass, figures of sailors, citizens, the arms of the painters' guild, a dragon, an eagle, or a head carved in wood. From the midst of such surroundings, at the corner of Garden Court Street and Bell Alley, rose the stately old mansion, with its neighbor, the Hutchinson house, a symbol of commercial success and social leadership.

The house was built, or possibly remodeled, by William Clark, a rich merchant and councillor, about 1712. It was demolished in 1833. Around the memory of this old house is a halo of romance, for about it surged the infuriated mob which attacked its neighbor, and within the walls was born an ancestor of the Marquis of Lorne, husband of Princess Louise; a grandchild of the builder died in poverty; here also lived the beautiful Agnes Surriage, Lady Frankland, whose story outrivals that of Cinderella.

She was the heroine of the Lisbon earthquake, when she saved Sir Harry's life at the risk of her own; of Bynner's novel bearing her name; of Dr. Nason's biography of Sir Harry; and of a poem by Oliver Wendell Holmes—

'Tis like some poet's pictured trance
His idle rhymes recite,—
This old New England-born romance
Of Agnes and the Knight.

Her father was a humble fisherman, whose little cottage stood on the Marblehead shore opposite the fort, and not far from the Fountain Inn, where Agnes first met her future husband.

After his death she lived part of the time at their country house in Hopkinton, and was there when the Revolution burst like a storm over the land. Being the widow of an officer of the Crown, her splendid equipage and style of living, surrounded as she was by ardent patriots, made her residence in the country so precarious that she applied for a pass to Boston, where she shortly arrived under the protection of an armed guard. Once more she occupied her fairy castle, which she opened to the wounded on that memorable seventeenth of June; and then fled, a refugee, never more to see her native land.

The last owner of the house, Samuel Ellis, married Caroline Matilda Orne Boyd Little, the daughter of his neighbor of the Hutchinson house. Realizing, when he moved from Boston, that he would never occupy the house again, and wishing to prevent it being occupied by others, or perhaps being put to meaner use like the Province House, he sold it with the understanding that it should at once be razed to the ground.

The following description of the Clark house is taken from the article by Mr. Henry Lee, in the *Proceedings* of the Massachusetts Historical Society, for the year 1881:

"Opposite the door was the ample fireplace with its classic mantel-piece, a basket of flowers and scroll-work in relief upon its frieze. On the right of the chimney-piece was an arched alcove lighted by a narrow window; on the left an arched buffet with a vaulted ceiling.

"The other three walls were divided into compartments by fluted pilasters of the Corinthian order, which supported the entablature with its dentilled cornice.

"The flutings and capitals of the pilasters, the dentils of the cornice, the vault and shelves of the buffet, were all heavily gilded. So far, as I said before, it was only a rich example of the prevalent style.

"The peculiar decoration consisted of a series of raised panels filling these compartments, reaching from the surbase to the frieze, eleven in all, each embellished with a romantic landscape painted in oil colors, the four panels opposite the windows being further enriched by the emblazoned escutcheons of the Clarks, the Saltonstalls, and other allied families.

"Beneath the surbase, the panels, as also those of the door, were covered with arabesques. The twelfth painting was a view of the house upon a horizontal panel over the mantel, and beneath this panel, inscribed in an oval, was the monogram of the builder, W. C. At the base of the gilded and fluted vault of the buffet was a painted dove."

The five panels represented by the illustrations are the only ones still existing. The colors are mellowed by age, browns and greens predominating. The first four are about five feet in height.

One of these panels (fig. 1) represents a mounted traveler approaching an inn embowered with great trees. The house is brown, the roof having a reddish tone, while the ancient sign hanging over the door, representing the Dog's Head in the Crock, has a green background, with light brown figures. The woman standing in the doorway is dressed in dark shades of blue and brown; the rider's coat is red, as are the distant figures; and his horse is reddish brown. The shield (Hubbard) is quartered gold and silver, over all a red bend with three golden lions. The crest is· a silver elephant's head and spear.

Another (fig. 2) shows a stately old castle on a precipitous hill, with smiling fields and distant mountains; at the foot of the cliff stand two men, and from the look of surprise on the face of the younger one in the cloak and wreath and the haughty air of the other as he points into the distance, one surmises that he is ordering his son to leave the ancestral roof—the castle on the cliff. The elderly man wears a red coat and brownish smallclothes, the other a red cap with a green wreath about it. Browns and greens predominate in the landscape, the mountains dissolving into misty blue.

The third panel (fig. 3), best of all in composition, drawing, and color, represents a sylvan retreat with a great forest in the background, varying in color from the delicate greens of the trees in the sunlight, to the deep somber tones of the shadowy depths of the forest. There are two romantic young people in the foreground, who are so absorbed in each other that they are oblivious of the passing of time or the dark clouds gathering over the treetops—producing an effect quite suggestive of Watteau. Their costumes, including the man's wig and the high headdress of the woman, obviously belong to the time of Queen Anne. The man is wearing a red coat and black boots, the lady a red upper garment with a blue skirt; she has dark brown hair and wears a white cap. The figures in the distance are red, as are the

2. PANEL FROM THE CLARK HOUSE

Courtesy of the Maine Historical Society, Portland, Maine.

deer. Shield (Saltonstall)—the eagles and bar in the coat-of-arms are black on a gold field; the scrolls are red. The crest is a reddish black pelican issuing from a golden crown, while the ribbons that hold the shield are also red.

1. PANEL WITH ESCUTCHEON FROM THE
CLARK HOUSE, BOSTON, MASSACHUSETTS

*Courtesy of the Maine Historical Society, Portland,
Maine.*

3. PANEL WITH ESCUTCHEON FROM THE
CLARK HOUSE, BOSTON

*Courtesy of Mrs. Frederick Gay, Brookline,
Massachusetts.*

4. PANEL WITH ESCUTCHEON FROM THE
CLARK HOUSE, BOSTON

*Courtesy of Mrs. Frederick Gay, Brookline,
Massachusetts.*

The fourth panel (fig. 4) has a great castle and other buildings in a light brown tone, with red roofs; in the foreground are trees, bushes, a cow and goat, nearly black in color, the yellowish fields shading to pinkish brown. To the right a man in a red cloak and riding a gray mule is approaching the castle. Shield (Clark)—the symbols in the coat-of-arms, a ragged staff and three balls, are black on a gold field. The crest is a silver swan with red bill and claws and black legs, having a gray olive branch in its mouth and surmounted by a black crown. The scrolls and ribbon are red. On each of the escutcheons the space between the outer and inner scrolls is dull blue lined with black.

The panel with the fourth coat-of-arms is missing, so that the series is not complete. The escutcheon, however, is believed to be that of the Whittingham family, with which the Clarks were connected.

The last panel (fig. 5) is a picture of the house, which was over the mantel. It shows a red brick building with roof balustrade, the doorway and windows outlined in white, with a pale blue sky above. An unusual feature is noticed in the narrow windows at each side, which lighted the alcoves by the fireplace. This picture is rather crudely

5. OVER-MANTEL PANEL FROM THE CLARK
HOUSE

painted, evidently by another hand. The subject bears a strong resemblance to the Warner house of Portsmouth, New Hampshire, which was built a few years later.

There is a tradition that William Clark brought a painter from London to decorate his parlor; and the technique and general characteristics of the work make it appear possible that this artist was R. Robinson, a decorator and mezzotint artist of considerable ability, who painted a series of wood panels in the house of a London merchant, as described by E. W. Tristram in the *Third Annual Volume* of the Walpole Society.

6. ROOM FROM "MARMION," STAFFORD COUNTY, VIRGINIA

Marmion[1]

THERE has recently been installed in the Metropolitan Museum of Art in New York City the paneled woodwork which formerly covered the walls of one of the principal rooms—parlor or dining-room—in the plantation mansion known as "Marmion," in Stafford County, Virginia. Some of these panels are decorated with fruit and flower designs, others with landscapes, and as they form a part of the wainscot they belong to the same group of house decorations as the panels from the Clark house, to which they bear a general resemblance. While only a few of the Clark panels are left, the entire woodwork of "Marmion" has been preserved, so that we have at least one perfect room of this character.

It is said that the original house was erected in 1674, by William Fitzhugh, whose will was probated in Stafford County in 1701, in which the property is devised to his son Thomas. It was afterwards purchased by George Lewis, a nephew of General Washington.

The room (fig. 6) is rectangular, with the end opposite the entrance extended into a sort of bay which accommodates the chimney-piece and a closet. The walls are

[1] Photographs by courtesy of The Metropolitan Museum of Art, New York City.

covered with large decorated panels, a dado, and an entablature supported by fluted Ionic pilasters which reach from floor to ceiling.

These pilasters flank both sides of doors, windows, chimney-piece, and panels. The paintings are neither signed nor dated, but features of the architectural details make it apparent that the woodwork belongs to the middle of the eighteenth century and that the decorations were painted at the time the room was finished.

The wall opposite the windows has three large upright panels about 32 by 48 inches in size, with a narrow one near the door. Two of these panels are coupled between the pilasters, with a corresponding section of dado which has a single panel the width of the two above, an arrangement also carried out at the left of the door beneath the landscape panels. Between the windows is a single panel framed with the pilasters of the windows and on the chimney-breast a small one about 30 inches square flanked by a narrow panel on each side and below. The opening of the fireplace is edged with yellow mottled marble arched at the top, enclosed by a molding of white marble.

The panels are painted a light tone of brown, the entablature (except the frieze), dado, and pilasters a dark rich shade of the same color mottled to represent veined marble. The special attraction of the room, however, consists of the decorations painted on the panels. The first two have baskets with rococo scroll

7. FRUIT AND FLOWER PANEL FROM "MARMION"

bases, filled with fruit and flowers glowing in soft tones of yellow, red, and green, with the rich golden harmonious effect of age. The next panel has a large urn on a marble base, draped with heavy festoons around the edges, on which rests a basket filled with roses and other flowers.

On the panel (fig. 7) between the windows appears a large cornucopia banded with dark color on a light ground, which is likewise filled with flowers and fruit, while around the horn is draped a delicate garland of roses and leaves. At the top of each of these fruit and flower panels hangs a festoon with a rose at the center, all in natural colors, light, fanciful, and attractive.

Each section of the dado has a large and rather heavy garland of leaves.

Scattered over the balance of the woodwork and the very narrow panels and at the top of the two large landscape panels are rococo scroll figures.

The flower and fruit figures show considerable skill and attention to fine details, and would seem to be a sufficient decoration for the room without the addition of the land-

8. LANDSCAPE PANELS FROM "MARMION"

scapes which now, at least, are dim and uncertain in appearance and on the whole rather inferior in quality.

The first of the landscapes (fig. 8) represents a mansion of the period, painted brown, showing an esplanade on the edge of a deep chasm with a ledge and trees beyond. In the distance there seem to be a river, low hills, and other houses. On the terrace are a man and a woman dressed in the style of the last half of the eighteenth century. They appear to be in earnest conversation, the woman with her left hand held as far away from the man as possible, apparently preventing him from taking something which she is holding, and for which he seems to be reaching. From around the corner of the building a small dog skips joyfully toward them as if in greeting.

In the shadows just beneath the terrace there lurks a dark figure who may be a husband or lover, and is watching the two upon the terrace. Just such a scene might Hogarth have painted.

The companion picture presents a view of a high cliff crowned by a medieval castle. At the foot of the cliff and in its shadow sits a man of large proportions, near whom are one or more travelers who are welcomed by a woman with outstretched hands, advancing from the door of an inn or tavern in the

9. OVER-MANTEL PANEL FROM "MARMION"

background. There are lofty trees with deep green foliage and in the distance can be seen a river and a wide valley between low hills, reminiscent of the Rhine and its castled crags. The picture over the mantel (fig. 9) has very decided Dutch characteristics and shows the perspective which belongs to the eighteenth century. The principal object is a windmill at the top of an arched rock of huge dimensions, with a castle along the left side. The rock is surrounded by water and there are sailboats all about. On the left towers an ornate portico with an equestrian statue placed on the peak of the pediment. In front are two persons who seem to be greeting each other. The scene is lighted by the pink rays of a sunset which bursts through dark gray clouds.

Near the two upper corners of this panel are two heads in dark monotone with rococo supports. The one on the left seems to represent a woman, while the other resembles a man, without the wigs of the period, and may be crude attempts of the artist to portray the master and mistress of the plantation. The small scene over the door (fig. 10) presents, apparently, a storm at sea with a ship in distress and a lighthouse, rather crudely executed. The landscapes were painted in thick dabs and are now seamed by fine lines like an old wrinkled piece of leather, as indistinct as if covered by a veil or a film of dust. The flower and fruit pieces present an entirely different technique, with a rather smooth, even surface, the figures clear and distinct.

The great difference seen in the technique of these two sets of paintings suggests that they were done by different persons of varying talent. It is also noticeable that the two large landscapes are not carried to the top of each panel, but end just under an arch of scroll figures, which does not appear on any of the other panels.

There is apparently only one thin coat of paint above these scrolls, so that the landscapes give the panels a *painted over* appearance, as if they were added at a later period, and cover any design previously painted there.

The scrolled arch also closely resembles one on the end of a Bavarian dower chest dated 1784—illustrated in color in *The Practical Book of Period Furniture* (Eberlein)—which suggests a Pennsylvania-German origin of these decorations, and that these scrolls belong to the end of the rococo period, about 1770 or later. This suggestion is strengthened by the close resemblance of the thin garland of roses to one painted on the wall panels of a peasant's house in the Tyrol (Holme, *Peasant Art in Austria and Hungary*).

NOTE

There is an interesting family tradition concerning the origin of these decorations, which nearly rivals the story of the young woodcarver who decorated "Whitehall" in Maryland.

According to the story the panels were painted by a Hessian soldier, who in 1782 was found, ill and starving, by the great-grandfather of the present owner, on the bank of the Potomac River, a short distance away. He was taken to the house and nursed back to health and strength, and out of gratitude for the kindness shown him, he decorated the panels, using paint which he made from the clay on the land. The figures on the terrace are said to be the dancing master and his wife, who were giving lessons in the family at the time.

11. ITALIAN LANDSCAPE. OVER-MANTEL PANEL IN THE WELLS HOUSE, NEAR MIDDLETOWN, CONNECTICUT

The Single Panel Group

IN the house of Mrs. Philip P. Wells, near Middletown, Connecticut, built in 1742, there is an over-mantel made from a single board (fig. 11), between fluted Doric pilasters which extend from floor to cornice, on which was painted many years ago an Italian landscape after the style of Claude Lorrain. It depicts a grove of trees beneath which cows are feeding; a partially ruined Corinthian portico; a sheet of water once blue but now a vivid green; a bridge of many arches leading to a building with a high tower. In the foreground facing the portico stand a lady and gentleman dressed in the style of the early eighteenth century, while near the grove is a group of peasants resting from their labors. One stands with a rake over his shoulder, another is a woman seated, opposite whom a man, likewise seated, seems to be playing on a musical instrument.

The prevailing tone is a greenish gray, due to the yellowing effects of time, so that the picture is a little indistinct in details, but the effect is pleasing and makes the chimney-piece the most decorative feature of the room.

This picture is supposed to have been painted by an Italian artist about the time the house was built, but it is without signature or date, and may be the work of the Italian Cornè, as the ruined section of wall and the arches above the door beneath

12. OVER-MANTEL PANEL FROM THE ALEXANDER KING HOUSE, SUFFIELD, CONNECTICUT

the portico closely resemble a similar section of wall near a cottage in one of the scenes in the Lindell-Andrews house in Salem, Massachusetts. If so, it was probably painted about 1812, when Cornè was in Providence, or after 1822, when he moved to Newport.

Among the single over-mantel panel pictures, one in the Alexander King house (fig. 12) in Suffield, Connecticut, built in 1764, claims special attention for its historic value, although the colors, now yellowed with age, are faint and thin after the manner of a washed drawing.

It was painted with oils on a single piece of wood, which, with the entire chimney-piece, is flanked on each side by fluted pilasters. In the foreground, on what appears to be a cliff, there is a high road, along which is being driven at full speed a black, oval-shaped coach, of the type built during the years 1815-1825. It is drawn by four brown horses, on one of which rides a postilion in red livery. Near by stands a house and a little farther along a countryman is leading a horse laden with sacks of grain.

Far below the cliff is seen a broad river or harbor, on which float black ships with white sails, with a picturesque wooded isle in the center, and toward the horizon low hills and scattering houses. Overhead is a buff sky, once white, with a dash of red

13. "GARDEN OF EDEN" PANEL IN THE ALLEN HOUSE, BROOKLYN, CONNECTICUT

along the horizon. The scene bears some resemblance to an old view of Richmond and the James River, as well as a scene on an old Zuber wall paper manufactured in Alsace-Lorraine about 1830, called the "Wonders of Nature." This paper depicts small detached American views, among which are the Natural Bridge in Virginia, Niagara Falls, West Point, and Boston Harbor.

In Brooklyn, Connecticut, and its vicinity are three wood over-mantel panels each having a landscape painted in oils. The largest of them is in the old Allen mansion (fig. 13) on the top of Allen's Hill. The house, a large, two-story building with a wide central hall, was erected in 1803, replacing an older one. Over the broad doorway is an ornate Venetian window, picturesque and imposing, as one gets a view of the white walls between the masses of roses and shade trees.

The panel is in the parlor and was made from a single board about five feet long and three wide. The scene represents a forest with trees of great girth having round bunches of leaves at the top. The largest tree is in the center, and on a limb of it sits a tawny mountain lion who seems to be rather calmly contemplating a graceful brown deer which, with head uplifted, is bounding away into the distance.

The sky, the deep rich greens of the foliage, and the brown of the tree trunks, have become darkened with age, which lends the colors an added richness. The scene is believed to represent the hill as it was when originally settled by the family, and to show the wild animals found there. Because of the presence of so many different animals, which do not show clearly in the photograph, it has been called the "Garden of Eden."

A similar panel is in the home of Mrs. Livesy (fig. 14) in the town of Brooklyn. This is a very narrow one with a large tree at each end and another in the center,

14. OVER-MANTEL PANEL IN THE LIVESY HOUSE, BROOKLYN, CONNECTICUT

while along the horizon are small ones all in a very orderly row. On the branches of the tree in the center can be seen a white, wise old owl, who is being closely observed by a bird on one side and a squirrel on the other. A hunter, dismounted from his white horse, is aiming his gun, perhaps at the deer toward which his dog is running. Just in front of the deer may be discerned the faint outlines of another animal, and on the extreme left, beyond the tree, stands a bear. The foliage is dull green, the other tones are reddish browns.

In the town of Canterbury stands an old house in which there is a panel about three feet square with a view of a town on the seashore (fig. 15). The houses are white with red roofs, and a church with a tall spire is seen above the treetops, against a background of green hills. Opposite the town lies an island with a tall white lighthouse; there are also several ships, one near the town being a man-of-war. Overhead is an orange-red sunset, and across the top is painted a dark canopy with hanging ends, looped up by a cord and tassels. The painter of this, as of the two preceding panels, is unknown.

Another landscape panel (fig. 16) represents the village green of Cheshire, Connecticut, with houses, people, carriages, and the Congregational Church, which was

15. PANEL IN THE PALMER HOUSE, CANTERBURY, CONNECTICUT

16. PANEL FROM CHESHIRE, CONNECTICUT, NOW IN THE CHESHIRE PUBLIC
LIBRARY

built in 1736, the panel probably dating from 1800 to 1825. The quaintness of coloring and drawing reminds one of "Amen Street" in the Tinker house in Lyme, although it differs in details, and is on the whole rather superior.

17. DOOR PANEL IN THE THAXTER HOUSE, HINGHAM, MASSACHUSETTS

The church is the prominent feature, its white walls and spire being in strong contrast to the brown and green background now dark with age. It is a typical New England village of a century ago.

The picture is believed to have been painted by Sylvester Hall, who was born in Wallingford, in the year 1778, the son of Elisha and Ann Hopkins Hall. According to tradition, he was an uneducated painter with wandering inclinations and a thirst for the grape, and left no other known example of his work.

This panel, which was originally over the fireplace in the Rufus Hitchcock house, is now in the Cheshire Public Library.

In Hingham, Massachusetts, are some small landscapes painted in oil on the panels of the wainscot at the end of one of the rooms in the old Thaxter mansion, which was built about 1680, and is now occupied by the Wompatuck Club. Over the mantel are two scenes, one above the other, on long narrow panels, while on each side are others on narrow vertical ones. On a door at the left (fig. 17) are two more scenes nearly square, almost covering its entire surface. They are supposed to represent local rural views, in which large trees and rather amateurishly sketched houses predominate. The original colors have changed to dull browns and yellows.

It is supposed they were painted about 1785-1787. As a decoration they make a pleasing variation from the white color of the wainscot which covers nearly the whole of the end of the room.

The pictures are attributed to a local artist, John Hazlitt (born in 1767, died 1837), who, with his father, the Rev. William Hazlitt, lived in the house a number of years prior to 1787, in which year he returned to England. He is said to have been a self-taught artist, who later became a very successful painter of miniatures abroad, even winning the praise of Sir Joshua Reynolds.

THE FRESCOES

WARNER HOUSE
CORNÈ AND HIS WORK
VALENTINE MUSEUM
CONNECTICUT RIVER VALLEY GROUP
AMERICAN LANDSCAPE GROUP
ALSOP HOUSE

26. SALEM HARBOR. PANEL BY CORNÈ IN EAST INDIA MARINE MUSEUM,
SALEM, MASSACHUSETTS

THE FRESCOES

Warner House

DIFFERING entirely from the paintings on the Clark panels in size and character, and in many respects more interesting, are the frescoes in the Warner House at Portsmouth, New Hampshire.

This house is probably the oldest of the Colonial mansions now existing in New England. It is a two-story brick structure with denticulated cornices and string courses, with walls eighteen inches thick, resting on massive foundations, the eastern end protected by clapboards. It has a gambrel roof with five dormer windows across the front with curved and pointed pediments alternating, balustrade and cupola, and two chimneys at each end with a high connecting wall between them. The wide entrance is surmounted by a curved pediment supported by fluted pilasters with carved Corinthian capitals. Over the massive door is a transom of thick, antique glass. The windows are high and narrow, those of the first story having arched lintels, those above being flat. A noticeable feature of the windows is the number and arrangement of the panes of glass; there are fifteen to each window, the upper sash having nine, while the lower one has but six. The same proportion is carried out in the dormer windows, as well as in the half-windows at the end. Within are deep window seats and paneled shutters. Around the fireplaces are antique picture tiles.

The house was built by Captain Archibald Macpheadris, a rich Scottish merchant, with brick imported from Holland. It was commenced in 1712 but was not finished until 1716, the year the furniture arrived from abroad, according to the bill of lading, which has been preserved. When the house was nearly completed, one of the cargoes of brick for the house was wrecked off the Isles of Shoals, but undaunted, the Captain ordered another shipload and pensioned the workmen for the ensuing year, while awaiting its arrival.

Captain Macpheadris was a member of the Royal Council and was the chief promoter of the iron works at Dover. He married Sarah Wentworth, one of the sixteen children of Lieutenant Governor John Wentworth. His daughter Mary, in 1754, married the Honorable Jonathan Warner, who was also a member of the Council until the Revolution.

On each floor of the Warner house are four rooms with a large hall running through the middle from front to rear, the lower hall being divided at the center by an arch

18. FRESCOES IN THE LOWER HALL OF THE WARNER HOUSE, PORTSMOUTH, NEW HAMPSHIRE

supported by fluted Doric pilasters, beyond which is the staircase. Beginning with the arch and covering the plastered wall above the paneled dado of the staircase is the series of remarkable frescoes, which, forming the most interesting single feature of the house, have made it famous. No records are extant, but it is believed that the scenes were painted when the house was built. Although showing signs of age, they are in excellent condition. For years they were covered with wall paper, four layers having accumulated, and while this was being removed, some sixty years ago, the picture of a horse's hoof was discovered. Further investigation revealed the entire horse and a rider who was supposed to represent Governor Phips. The remaining sections of paper were then removed, and when all had been taken off, there appeared before the astonished eyes of the household a series of pictures covering the entire end of the hall from the first to the second story. One section was devoted to a farmyard scene, in which a woman at the spinning-wheel is interrupted by an enormous eagle which has captured a chicken and is flying away with it, while the ever-faithful dog springs forward to the attack. Then at the upper end of the staircase was discovered a Scriptural scene: Abraham offering Isaac as a sacrifice. On each side of the large window at the head of the staircase appeared the figure of an Indian chief, standing beneath a rich canopy with dark red curtains.

The paintings, covering several hundred square feet of surface, were now revealed in all their original freshness and beauty, save for a few scars. No one at the time had ever heard of them, and they were as complete a surprise to an old lady of eighty, who

20. SIR WILLIAM PEPPERELL

21. TWO INDIAN CHIEFS

19. ABRAHAM AND ISAAC

FRESCOES IN THE WARNER HOUSE

had been familiar with the house from childhood, as to her granddaughter, the little girl whose bright eyes were the first to make the discovery of the horse's hoof.

In the first scene (fig. 18), which begins in the lower hall next the arch, the woman spinning is dressed in the conventional Puritan style in a blue gown, with white hood, collar, and apron. The dog is white with brown back and ears; the eagle is nearly black, while the hawk and the chicken are light brown shading to yellowish white. The sky is yellow in tone and the ground shades from a rich green to a dark brown.

Above and beyond this picture, filling the balance of the wall space on this side, is the Scriptural scene (fig. 19). On a mountain height beneath a large greenish brown tree is seen Isaac, partially dressed in a white garment and kneeling on a pile of fagots, ready for the sacrifice, while Abraham towers over him, a tall, commanding figure; his right hand raises a sword above his head, while his left rests on the boy's shoulder. He has white hair and beard and is clad in a blue garment nearly covered by a red cloak. On his feet are buskins which reach to the knees. Behind the tree is seen the black ram. Near Abraham's feet, on the edge of a cliff, on which various plants are growing, is a large urn, from which issue fire and smoke. To the left of these figures, the blue sky is nearly covered by a great tawny cloud, in the midst of which is seen the angel, dressed in a brown garment, with brown flowing locks and white wings. He points to Abraham with his left hand, as if commanding him to spare the child. In the lower section of the scene are the two men with the ass, incongruous in clothes of Queen Anne's time, with a castellated building in the middle distance. The deep, rich tones of the picture are relieved by the brilliant colors of a small bird with red and white plumage, poised just above Abraham's sword.

It is an impressive and dramatic scene, at the supreme moment of action.

"And Abraham built an altar there, and laid the wood in order, and bound Isaac his son, and laid him on the altar upon the wood.

"And Abraham stretched forth his hand, and took the knife to slay his son.

"And the angel of the Lord called unto him out of heaven, and said, Abraham, Abraham: and he said, Here am I.

"And he said, Lay not thine hand upon the lad. . . .

"And Abraham lifted up his eyes, and looked, and behold behind him a ram caught in a thicket by his horns: and Abraham went and took the ram, and offered him up for a burnt offering in the stead of his son."

On the opposite side of the hall is the first picture discovered (fig. 20), a full-length portrait of an officer mounted upon a prancing, high-spirited steed. Although rather large for his horse, the rider makes a picturesque figure. He is dressed in a rich, embroidered scarlet coat, a long white wig, on which is placed a black cocked hat with a large white plume, white neckcloth, ruffled shirt and cuffs, buff smallclothes, and high black boots. His right hand rests upon a holster on which is a large letter P beneath a crown. The flesh tones are wonderfully clear and lifelike, and there is a good deal of expression and character to the features. In the distance, beneath a blue sky, there are mountains, green fields, and a village, the foreground being a deep tone of brown. To the right and left are dark masses of foliage, the whole relieved, as in the other scene, by the bright flashing colors of a small bird chased by a hawk, while another calmly rests on a branch of a dead tree directly in front of the horse.

Although this has been called an equestrian portrait of Governor Phips, it is more probably one of Sir William Pepperell, the hero of the capture of Louisburg in 1745. By comparing this portrait with the officer on an iron fireback cast at that time, and now the property of the Essex Institute, it will be seen that the pose of both rider and horse is similar. The initials W. P. and the date 1745, together with a long line of shackled prisoners under the officer on the fireback, sufficiently identify that figure as Pepperell.

The fact that the costume of the officer in the fresco belongs to the latter half of the century—years after the death of William Phips—also tends to confirm this theory.

The picture of the two Indian chiefs (fig. 21), while dimmer and considerably scarred, is in a more prominent position than the others, as it faces the stairs. The chiefs stand beneath a canopy painted above the arch of the window, from which fall draperies, looped up on either side. The colors are dull reds and browns, shading to black. The arched ceiling of the hall is sky blue, giving the impression that the canopy has been erected out of doors in a forest. The figures undoubtedly represent two of the four great Mohawk chieftains who went to England with Peter Schuyler, the first mayor of Albany, in 1709-1710. The chiefs were received in royal style, riding in state to St. James's, where they were presented to Queen Anne, who received them with royal honors. While in London they lived in sumptuous apartments, and were entertained at the tables of noblemen and statesmen. They were the sensation of the day, and mobs followed them whenever they rode about the city. Their full-length portraits were painted by Verelst. One was called "Emperor of the Mohawks," the others "Kings."

The Indians in the Warner frescoes are close copies of two of the four portraits painted in England, although showing small differences in details.

The figure on the left of the window corresponds with Verelst's painting of Etow Oh Koam, King of the River Nation, Turtle Tribe. That on the right is John, King of the Generethgarich, Wolf Tribe.

27. CANTON FACTORIES. FIREBOARD BY CORNÈ IN EAST INDIA MARINE MUSEUM

Cornè and His Work

IN 1799 General E. H. Derby, a merchant of Salem, Massachusetts, gave free passage in his ship *Mount Vernon* to Michele Felice Cornè, an Italian refugee.

Cornè was a Neapolitan by birth and a prolific painter of considerable ability. His work included portraits, imitations of Hogarth, and even tavern signs, but it was for his paintings of ships and for his landscapes that he became famous. He had a keen instinct for popularity and made the most of the opportunities which arose to bring him fame. Thus, on the news of the *Constitution's* victory over the *Guerrière,* "quickly seizing a broad canvas, as large as he could conveniently get into an exhibition room, he dashed off a picture of the combat . . . with striking effect, free from all unnecessary details but accurate enough to bear the criticisms of nautical men who flocked to see it. The success of the exhibition led him to paint the 'Boarding of the *Frolic,*' and the 'Surrender of the *Java* to the *Constitution*'—scenes vividly portrayed and hailed with acclamation.''[1]

In his mural paintings "his custom was not to paint directly on the wall, but to cover the whole surface with wide strips of white paper, joining the edges neatly and putting it on like ordinary wall paper. On this he first sketched his subject in charcoal and lead pencil, and then washed it in with water-colors, using in the foreground

[1] Mason, *Reminiscences of Newport.*

opaque colors laid on with size, which gave his work more body than he could secure in any other way.'"[1]

Cornè stayed in Salem for several years after his arrival, and then moved to Boston, remaining until 1822, when, finding that the public was losing interest in his work, he retired to Newport, where he lived until his death in 1845.

Among the mural paintings attributed to Cornè are those in the Oak Hill mansion in Peabody. The pictures are about three feet square and are painted on canvas which is fastened to the chimney-breast by carved moldings. The one in the drawing-room (fig. 22) is composed of a group of several people and children beneath a large tree close by a thatched cottage, from which a path winds into the distance through an open gate, toward hills crowned with what may be fortified cities. The central figure is an old woman mounted on an ass, carrying a staff and holding an infant in her arms, while a girl in a high-crowned bonnet is fastening her hood at the chin. Another woman, of a rather severe countenance, is holding open

22. PAINTING IN THE DRAWING-ROOM OF THE OAK HILL MANSION, PEABODY, MASSACHUSETTS

the gate. A child is playing with a dog, while two others—a boy and a girl—standing in front of a young man seated on a bench, who has been reading from an open book, are apparently bidding each other good-bye.

There is a blue sky with yellow clouds, the cottage is brown with yellow thatch covering the roof, and the fields and trees are in contrasting shades of green. The central figure wears a red garment, the others, dresses of green, blue, and brown.

The picture in the room across the hall is similar (fig. 23), having a family group about the open door of a thatched cottage beneath a large overhanging tree. The young wife is presenting an infant to her husband, seated on a bench by the door with farm tools about him, for the paternal kiss. Another woman is knitting; a third caresses a child; a boy is feeding two young pigs; and from the doorway an elderly person is watching the scene. The colors correspond with those in the other picture, browns and greens predominating.

[1] Mason, *Reminiscences of Newport*.

Although the drawing is faulty the figures are effectively grouped, the rich, harmonizing colors obscuring minor defects. In contrast to the white woodwork of one room and the dark, mahogany tones of the other, they form the most attractive decorative feature in each.

Another painting attributed to Cornè is the fresco on the plaster ceiling of the cupola of the Pickman-Derby-Brookhouse mansion (figs. 24, 25) in Salem, erected about 1790, and now in the garden of the Essex Institute. The ceiling is in the form of a low, wide dome springing from a denticulated cornice, and on the narrow strip at the bottom, beneath a grayish blue sky partly covered with white and reddish brown clouds which are touched with sunset hues of yellow and gold above a pink horizon, are painted the ships of the Derby fleet.

23. PAINTING IN ANOTHER ROOM OF THE OAK HILL MANSION

Well drawn and well grouped, with flags flying and white sails shining against the dark, rocky headlands, the ships make a stirring picture.

On the right shore, close to the water's edge, there is a medieval city with great towers and high walls and many houses, which are reflected in the water. In the foreground are ships and boats, with fishermen in the nearest ones drawing in great nets.

Although none of these paintings are signed, the general feeling and character of them, as well as the pigment and colors used, so closely resemble Cornè's known work—notably the Sullivan Dorr house in Providence—that there can be little doubt of their authorship.

There is a small panel picture belonging to the East India Marine Museum in Salem (fig. 26) which bears Cornè's signature and the date 1803. It is supposed to represent Salem harbor, with the Neck in the distance. At the left is a woman dressed in a white Empire gown seated on a rocky cliff overlooking the sea, with arms outspread as if in welcome. A ship with all sails set is seen putting to sea, while a rowboat filled with men seems to be following. On each side are cupids holding the ends of a ribbon on which are painted the words "East India Marine Hall," which were added by Samuel

Bartol in 1825. There is greenish blue sky with gray clouds tipped with white: the water reflects the colors of the sky. The ship, sails, and rocks are in brown tones. The coloring is good, the drawing of the ship excellent, the figure of the woman being the weakest point.

24. FRESCOED CEILING IN THE CUPOLA OF THE PICKMAN-DERBY-BROOKHOUSE
MANSION, SALEM, MASSACHUSETTS
Courtesy of The Essex Institute, Salem, Massachusetts.

In the Museum is also a fireboard painted by Cornè and representing the Canton Factories as seen from the water front (fig. 27). The sky is now light brown in tone shading to dark gray, the buildings light yellow or red. The ground and water are brown, the latter shading almost to black in the foreground. The two native boats on the right are brown with yellow sterns decorated with red. The flags—Danish, Spanish, United States, Swedish, and British—denote the countries represented by resident consuls.

These two examples of Cornè's work are given to show his style, although they are not wall decorations.

The most important frescoed or painted wall decorations in Salem are those on the walls of the hall in the Lindell-Andrews-Perkins house.[1] The scenes were painted free-hand on a covering surface of blank paper instead of on the plaster, a method which indicates these frescoes as probably Cornè's work, painted while he was a resident of the city.

25. FRESCOED CEILING IN THE CUPOLA OF THE PICKMAN-DERBY-BROOKHOUSE
MANSION

Courtesy of The Essex Institute, Salem, Massachusetts.

The paper is like thin cardboard, brittle and broken with age, the varnished paint forming a thin skin which is cracked exactly like that of a very old oil painting. Ridges of paint and brush marks are clearly seen. The bold effects of color and composition give a touch of fascination to the scenes. The colors are natural, with soft greens and browns of myriad tints, while over all spreads the effulgence of a golden sky. Many of the green tones in the pictures, such as those of water and mountains, as well as the brownish yellow of the sky and clouds (doubtless blue and white originally), are probably due to the effects of the yellow varnish, which also subdues the original brightness like a veil.

[1] Photographs by courtesy of The Essex Institute, Salem, Massachusetts.

28. FRESCO IN THE HALL OF THE LINDELL-ANDREWS-PERKINS
HOUSE, SALEM, MASSACHUSETTS

29. FRESCO IN THE HALL OF THE LINDELL-ANDREWS-PERKINS
HOUSE

On the right of the entrance to the hall (fig. 28) are lofty mountains, the largest one towering a greenish gray mass in the center, with sharp peaks like those of the Alps. Beneath the mountains are masses of brown rocks and trees, while a bridge of one great span stretches across a stream of greenish water with a shallow, foamy water-

fall and silvery, swirling ripples below. On the bridge are two men on horseback. In strong contrast to the dark clouds and shadows is the golden glow of the sky overhead.

Opposite this scene stands an old half-timbered, thatched cottage (fig. 29), surrounded by the tall trees, with a placid stream in front and to the right a ruined wall partially overgrown with trees. Beyond this section is a mill or fortified house with a bridge over a stream, in one of the windows of which a woman is kneeling.

The painting at the head of the stairs (fig. 30) depicts a cottage on the bank of a stream which winds away in the distance. In the foreground a woman is seated on a log, and beside her are two children.

Down the stairway tumbles a great waterfall (fig. 31), the outlet of a quiet river in the upper

30. FRESCO AT THE HEAD OF THE STAIRS IN THE LINDELL-ANDREWS-PERKINS HOUSE

hall. On the left, a cottage is almost hidden in a dark grove of trees, which extend along the river bank in cloudlike masses of lighter green. Two men are paddling a boat down the river, and beyond them is a long bridge leading to another scene with a greenish yellow sky, rock masses, tall trees, and rolling fields above a green lake.

On the right of the scene is a precipitous, tree-crowned hill (fig. 32), down which a hunter is leading his horse, while two others are riding madly after hounds which have surrounded a fox. One hunter has a blue coat, another a white one, a third a red one, all having yellow breeches. It is a lively scene, vibrating with action. One almost hears the baying of the hounds and the cheery calls of the hunters, as they close in on the fox.

31. FRESCO DOWN THE STAIRWAY OF THE LINDELL-ANDREWS-PERKINS HOUSE

Opposite this scene is, in many respects, the most important one of all (fig. 33). In this there is a thatched cottage with brick walls partially covered with stucco, over-hanging and surrounding which are rich dark green masses of foliage, which throw it into strong relief. Beyond the cottage, on a lower level, are the pale green tops of young forest trees, which stretch away to the ocean, the latter partially enclosed by a distant headland. The dark clouds above dissolve into a golden tint. In the cottage doorway are grouped three women and two children, who with anxious faces are gazing at a man dressed only in a shirt and trousers, his right hand grasping a staff, while his left points to a ship which is fast sinking in the angry waters of the distant sea. The

33. THATCHED COTTAGE. FRESCO IN THE HALL OF THE
LINDELL-ANDREWS-PERKINS HOUSE

32. HUNTING SCENE. FRESCO IN THE HALL OF THE LINDELL-
ANDREWS-PERKINS HOUSE

figures are so well drawn, the action so dramatic, the colors so rich, that this scene surpasses the others in interest. From the fact that the man wears pantaloons, the pictures were probably painted not earlier than 1800-1810, approximately the time when long trousers were introduced into this country. This strengthens the probability of their being the work of Cornè.

Further along the wall is a simple, peaceful idyl of pastoral life (fig. 34), with grazing sheep, herders, and a man standing by his horse.

The most important and ambitious series of frescoes by Cornè now extant adorns the mansion in Providence built in 1800 by Sullivan Dorr, a native of Boston, on land purchased from the family of Roger Williams. The house was designed by John Holden Greene, who is supposed to have been the architect employed by Alexander Pope for his villa at Twickenham. The owner was the father of Thomas Wilson Dorr, that brilliant and romantic but unfortunate figure in Rhode Island's history, who for a time was the people's governor of the state, and the leader of their party in the contest for equal suffrage, known as Dorr's Rebellion, in 1842.

01. PASTORAL SCENE. FRESCO IN THE HALL OF THE
LINDELL-ANDREWS-PERKINS HOUSE

The house, a large square building with a hall through the center, stands on a terrace above the street, surrounded by trees, a lawn, and a garden. The frescoes, which cover the walls of the parlor and upper and lower halls, were painted by Cornè during the years 1812-1815, or shortly after he is supposed to have painted frescoes in the Hancock house in Boston. The medium used was some kind of water color which was applied directly to the plaster. In the parlor the paintings are light in tone with a dull, almost chalky, finish, while in the hall a coat of varnish gives an additional luster and greater depth of color.

The scenes comprise ancient castles, crumbling palaces, classical ruins, ships, soldiers, people in gay colors, in the picturesque dress of the period; scenes in the tropics, with large birds of brilliant plumage; a northern winter; great masses of rocks and trees with dark green foliage; bright flowers in glowing colors, full of life and detail, with pose so natural they seem to be growing there. Whatever his faults in drawing, Cornè's colors are harmonious, and the scenes, which never repeat themselves, are delightfully decorative and effective.

Opposite the chimney-piece in the parlor the wall presents a large, unbroken surface about 8 by 20 feet between ceiling and dado, and here was painted the principal scene (frontispiece). It evidently represents the Bay of Naples,[1] with the threatening mass of Vesuvius in the distance. On the left are the frowning brown walls and towers of a huge castle which rises from the water's edge, while beyond it a lighthouse tower rises from the protecting wall of the inner harbor. Beyond stretches the gray and greenish water of the Mediterranean, from which rise gentle hills with green slopes and clustering villages, terminating in the purple crest of the volcano. The harbor is dotted with men-of-war flying the American flag of fifteen stars and stripes, used in the War of 1812, a sloop-of-war flying the British flag, and a number of the picturesque native boats.

35. ISLAND CASTLE. FRESCO BY CORNÈ IN THE PARLOR OF THE SULLIVAN DORR HOUSE, PROVIDENCE, RHODE ISLAND

Beneath the walls of the fortress are various groups of people; men fishing; an officer in the stern of a barge waving a hand in farewell; two women in pink Empire dresses and a girl in brown are standing on the reddish colored pier in the foreground, near whom are several men dressed in yellow, brown, and purple smallclothes with low-crowned beaver hats. In the midst of this group stands a martial figure in a red

---

[1] This probably bears a close resemblance to the panorama of the Bay of Naples which Cornè painted in Salem in 1809. It is thus mentioned by William Bentley in his diary:

"Dec. 1st 1809. Went with my young females HC. HH and MW. to see Cornè's Bay of Naples. Found it only a copy of the Common plates at the entrance neither showing the City nor Basin and without one stroke of originality. The Claim on the public notice was from a display of the American Ship Constitution dressed in flags of all nations with the six Gun boats lent by the King of Naples in the affair of Preble ag. Tripoli. Just such a parade he made of Columbus and his egg which proved, as this painting, to be only on a larger scale, the Etching of Hogarth, without the addition of a single stroke of the pencil."

uniform and a high plumed hat. Above the highest tower floats a white flag with a device in red.

On the next section of wall around the corner (fig. 35) can be seen a low island surrounded by a wall, above which rises a structure which may represent the Castello

36. CLIFF SCENE. FRESCO BY CORNÈ IN THE PARLOR OF THE SULLIVAN DORR HOUSE

dell' Ovo. It is connected with the mainland by a causeway. Three soldiers stand guard on the outer wall. Near by are fishermen drawing in their nets, while feluccas, their graceful, pointed sails raised, are cruising about.

Another scene (fig. 36) presents a great mass of dark brown ledges with a gray castle on the central height, while above and around it grow trees and shrubbery. Down a narrow pathway in the cliffs is seen a file of soldiers in cocked hats, with muskets on their shoulders, marching toward the shore. At the foot of the promontory some men are hauling up a skiff. In the far distance are the walls and towers of a city. Long lines of white-capped breakers surge in from the sea and dash into masses of foam upon the brown rocks. On the ledge in the foreground there is a group of four fisher folk, two men and two women. One woman wears a red bodice, the other a blue one; the man sprawling near them is dressed in white, while the other, who is standing, is garbed in brown and white. Apparently they are undisturbed by the military demonstration not far away.

37. OVER-MANTEL FRESCO BY CORNÈ IN THE PARLOR OF THE SULLIVAN DORR HOUSE

The next scene is over the mantel (fig. 37) and represents a ruined gateway or portico, of which there is left only an entablature supported by slender columns which in turn rest on great arches of solid masonry. Through the larger of these can be seen a narrow city street with high walls spanned by an arched bridge. On the left, in contradistinction to the ruins, are more modern houses, ledges of rock, and pale green trees. To the right circles a wall of many tiers of arches suggesting an amphitheater.

Between two of the windows there is a grayish brown fountain partially ruined (fig. 38), with a bust above a gargoyle in the form of a human head from which spurts a jet of water. At its side grows a solitary tree, and on the rocks in front stands a man with a fishnet and basket, gazing toward the fountain.

Another small wall space has a narrow panel in subdued tones of grays and browns, the trees and narrow tongues of low-lying land and their reflections in the placid water, looking as if veiled in mist. In the foreground a weary traveler, or very old man who leans upon a staff, is walking up a rustic bridge which rises sharply toward the fringe of trees on the opposite side.

In the halls the character of the scenes varies, the colors are deep and rich, occasionally even somber, the prevailing tones being a deep reddish brown, yellow, and green. The leaves are generally painted in dark masses, on which they are outlined by hooks and loops in a thin light shade, just as white paint is sometimes used over dark water color, for high lights. The pigment is thick and shows brush marks, and has the appearance of a thick skin where it peels from the wall. Each subject is a unity, although they all join together in a continuous series.

One scene (fig. 39) has a high expanse of sky, a broad sheet of water crossed by a causeway and a wooden bridge, a tongue of land in the foreground with masses of flowers and bushes, and trees of rich foliage to right and left. In the foreground are two hunters. One of them is aiming at a flock of flying birds, while the other is loading his gun with the assistance of a ramrod. The colors are rich greens, browns, and grays.

Another (fig. 40) has a grove of trees, a thatched cottage, near which is a row of slender pointed cedars, masses of rocks, a pool from which flows a gurgling stream, mountains, and at the side of a winding highway an inn with a signpost swinging from a tall pole; near by a one-horse chaise is being driven leisurely along.

Under the staircase is an old-fashioned winter scene (fig. 41), cold white and gray, with a figure in red chopping the ice at the edge of a stream, while another carries a load of wood on his back, and men in a sleigh drawn by black horses approach the house.

In sharp contrast with this is a scene that has all the glow, warmth, and brilliance of the tropics (fig. 42). Hunters assisted by brown natives are shooting birds of large size resembling pheasants, some of them red and white, others blue and red. The man beneath the palm tree wears a blue coat and a white, low-crowned beaver hat. Then are seen (fig. 43) a large greenish white waterfall,

38. RUINED FOUNTAIN. FRESCO BY CORNÈ IN PARLOR OF THE SULLIVAN DORR HOUSE

trees, and exotic plants on a high brown cliff, down which a sprightly cascade dashes to lose itself in a pool of greenish water below, near which two men are standing; overhead is a buff-colored sky. There is a brown ruin (fig. 44) overgrown with masses of trees on a hill near by, overlooking a river or bay, on the opposite shore of which is a group of houses square and flat. From the midst of the town rises a dome proclaiming a cathedral or a mosque. The red and blue clothes of the men in the foreground break the monotony of the brown and yellow tones. Then follows another peaceful, bucolic scene (fig. 45) with a noble ruin, great trees, and a little cottage toward which a man leads a horse.

Extending up the staircase (fig. 46) is a mass of beautiful flowers carefully drawn even to minute details. Among them can be distinguished red and yellow hollyhocks, white snowballs, roses, purple lilacs, with stalks and leaves in many shades of green, all so natural that they seem to be actually growing there, ready to bend and nod with each passing breeze. In fact, the beauty and brilliance of these flowers make this

39. HUNTING SCENE. FRESCO BY CORNÈ IN THE HALL OF THE SULLIVAN DORR HOUSE

section one of the most attractive in the halls. On a buff background above the flowers rises a row of poplar trees of somber green, which reach to the ceiling above. At the head of the staircase is another ruined palace (fig. 47) in a setting of trees, with water on both sides and, in front, rocks, trees, and a group of people.

This remarkable series of romantic foreign landscapes ends with a moonlight scene (fig. 48), the soft half-light from a full moon, of a silvery grayish green color, bathing with its soft radiance the water of a harbor, with luxuriant trees, and the grim walls of an ancient castle at the water's edge; and throwing into black shadow a sloop with its reflection, as it sails along the shore.

To Cornè have also been attributed the frescoes in "The Mount," a pretentious mansion built about 1812 in Bristol, Rhode Island, by James DeWolf, an adventurous sailor and privateersman who became a wealthy merchant and coffee-planter.

The house was destroyed by fire some years ago, and unfortunately no adequate pictures of the frescoes are in existence. These represented episodes from "Paul and Virginia" and tropical scenes of the owner's plantations.

40. PASTORAL SCENE. FRESCO BY CORNÈ IN THE HALL OF THE SULLIVAN DORR HOUSE

41. WINTER SCENE. FRESCO BY CORNÈ UNDER THE STAIRCASE
OF THE SULLIVAN DORR HOUSE

42. TROPICAL SCENE. FRESCO BY CORNÈ IN THE SULLIVAN DORR
HOUSE

43. THE WATERFALL. FRESCO BY CORNÈ IN THE SULLIVAN
DORR HOUSE

44. THE RUIN. FRESCO BY CORNÈ IN THE SULLIVAN DORR HOUSE

45. BUCOLIC SCENE. FRESCO BY CORNÈ IN THE SULLIVAN
DORR HOUSE

46. FLORAL FRESCO BY CORNÈ
UP THE STAIRCASE IN THE SULLIVAN
DORR HOUSE

47. RUINED PALACE. FRESCO BY CORNÈ AT HEAD OF STAIR-
CASE IN THE SULLIVAN DORR HOUSE

48. MOONLIGHT SCENE. FRESCO BY CORNÈ IN THE SULLIVAN
DORR HOUSE

49. ACHILLES CIRCLING THE WALLS OF TROY. FRESCO IN THE VALENTINE
MUSEUM, RICHMOND, VIRGINIA

Valentine Museum

AN entirely different style of decoration is seen in three small surviving panels
over doors in the Valentine Museum in Richmond, Virginia, the residence of
the late Mann S. Valentine, and one of the finest houses of its day in the city,
having been erected from plans by the architect Robert Mills in 1812.

The subjects of the panels are scenes from the Iliad and show the figures of goddesses, warriors, and fiery steeds in heroic action before the walls of Troy. These
figures are drawn in outline on the plaster with an effect not unlike that of modern
etchings.

It is this style of execution without color that makes them different from all other
contemporary frescoes in this country.

The drawing is exquisite and has all the life, vigor, and beauty of the outline drawings seen on Greek vases in museums. They are, in fact, practically perfect copies of
Flaxman's familiar outline illustrations of the Iliad, published first in Rome in 1792
and in England the year following.

It is thought that the other wall panels in this room, as well as those in the Monu-
mental Church in Richmond (erected in 1811), were also decorated in this style, although no trace of them now exists.

One of the surviving panels represents Hera and Athene going to the assistance of
the Greeks; another shows Polydamus advising Hector to retire from the trenches;
and the third panel is Achilles (fig. 49) circling the walls of Troy, with Hector's body
at the tail of his chariot.

Who drew these copies is not known, even tradition having failed to weave a story
around them.

53. PANEL IN THE "EAST ROOM" OF THE JAYNES HOUSE, EAST SETAUKET, LONG ISLAND

Connecticut River Valley Group

THE frescoes of the Connecticut River Valley form a special group, which includes rooms in Plymouth and Marlboro, Vermont; Saco, Maine, Bernardston and Deerfield, Massachusetts; Washington and Old Lyme, Connecticut; and the Jaynes homestead in East Setauket, Long Island. They probably were painted between the years 1782 and 1820.

They are unique in design and treatment and seem to be a native development from an old household art which until recently flourished in certain sections of this country. It might be said of these frescoes, in fact, that they came, like Pandora's troubles, from a box, the brightly ornamented dower chest of the Pennsylvania "Dutch," who settled in this country during the first half of the eighteenth century, bringing with them their arts and crafts, which were a racial inheritance from untold generations. Many designs in the frescoes are practically reproductions of those painted on their dower chest fronts and glassware, and scratched upon their pottery, or stitched into their embroideries, readily suggesting the possibility that some artist-decorator in their midst adapted these designs for wall decorations, as they are found in this group of houses.

That the decorators of these Connecticut Valley houses were of German origin is further suggested by the use of the Prussian eagle in some of the frescoes, and by the fact that much of this work was done in stencil, which seems to have been introduced into this country by the settlers in Pennsylvania.

Still older motifs are found, some almost identical with designs found in Pompeii.

The common origin of all these designs is indicated by the occurrence of the same motif in various rooms. Among these repetitions occurs the festooned drapery figure with cord and tassels which is seen in the Jaynes, Tinker, and Bernardston rooms; the vertical looped vine of the Jaynes house and the Red House; the diamond pattern seen in Bernardston as well as in the Gray house in Lyme; the arched dado, so prominent in the Red House, the two houses in Lyme, and in Bernardston; the delicate basket of cherries or flowers on very stiff stalks in Marlboro and Deerfield; as well as tulips, fuchsias, roses, and a host of small figures interspersed here and there.

The majority of these rooms show a preponderance of free-hand work, while three only (Marlboro, Plymouth, and Cromwell) show stencil work exclusively.

The frescoes of this group present a very unusual aspect, whether collectively or singly. When viewed from across the room they have the appearance of old Flemish tapestry, not only those pieces in which faded greenish blues and grays predominate, but the bright-colored ones as well, with red and yellow tones. The resemblance is greatly increased by the border which surrounds each section of fresco.

While probably not intended in any sense to be replicas of tapestry or silk brocade hangings, their form and style may have been influenced by the embroidered pieces of all kinds which these people produced; nevertheless, although probably a mere coincidence, the design in the Jaynes house and the Red House (minus the emblems), consisting of vertical looped vines, which form wreaths, is almost identical with the pattern of the tapestry hanging on the walls of Marie Antoinette's bedroom in Fontainebleau.

THE RED HOUSE

IN the town of Washington, Connecticut, there is a house of historic interest, built in 1772, known as the Red House. During the Revolution it is said to have been the home of two brothers, Amos and Lemuel Stone, one a Whig, the other a Tory.

It is said that the Tory brother, to show his loyalty to England, had a frieze painted on the walls of his parlor with designs of the British flag and men-of-war. The other chose the eagle with the other designs as shown in the illustrations of his parlor, which for years were covered with wall paper. The latter are the only frescoes which can at present be seen, as the paintings on the walls of the Tory brother's room were destroyed or papered over long ago. That room, however, is wainscotted throughout with especially fine paneling, which is in its original condition. The present owner has restored the house and has preserved this very ornate room, which is unusually interesting and has some historical importance as well. On a buff background are painted, with unvarnished tempera on the plaster, vertical rows of wreath-like loops and twining vines in black, with red roses at the points of intersection (fig. 50). In the center of each loop the figure of a white stag with proudly tossed head alternates vertically and horizontally with the national seal, a white eagle shaded into black, one foot holding an olive branch, the other a bunch of arrows, its head surrounded by a circle of thirteen stars. This heraldic device was accepted by Congress in 1782, which places the date of the frescoes as not earlier than that year. Around each section of the walls is a narrow border of vines and roses, which also passes over the tops of the doors in a double row. Between two windows, from dado to ceiling, is a narrow panel with a slender vine arch-

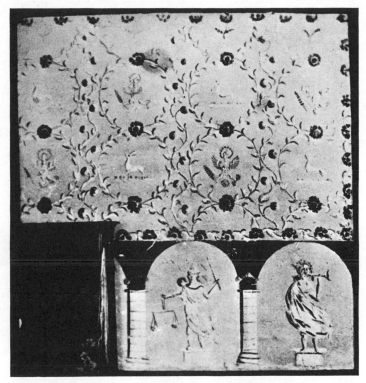

50. FRESCO IN THE PARLOR OF THE RED HOUSE, WASHINGTON, CONNECTICUT

ing to right and left, each branch with a fruit or flower at the end, between which are short sprays of leaves. At the base is a square panel (fig. 51) on which is emblazoned the black eagle of Prussia and the Rhine provinces, crowned, holding scepter and globe in its talons. Owing probably to either ignorance or carelessness, the artist made the heads of both the American and Prussian eagles face to the right instead of to the left, and also omitted the shield from the breast. The thirteen stars above the American eagle also should have been combined in the form of a six-pointed star surrounded by clouds, instead of being placed in a circle about the eagle's head. Over one series of this emblem are the words "Federal Union." This is an almost unbelievable combination, for that time, of the emblems of America and Britain's allies, the Germans, and surely could not have been painted there during the war. The Prussian eagle answers, however indirectly, as a signature of the artist, as it is very unlikely that anyone not of Teutonic origin would have used that emblem; and thus there seems to be here recorded a fact which gives some semblance of truth to the many traditions about the painting of our old frescoes and panel pictures by Hessians.

There is no chimney-piece, as the flat wall extends across that end of the room above the mantel, the usual arrangement at that period. Extending from the floor to the

51. FRESCO BETWEEN THE WINDOWS IN RED HOUSE

52. FRESCO OF WARRIORS IN THE RED HOUSE

height of the mantel is a dado, divided into many small panels or niches by columns which support maroon arches. In these spaces are painted mythological figures, such as Neptune with crown and trident, and Justice blindfolded, with scales in her right hand and in her left an upraised sword; another, in classical drapery, is blowing a trumpet; still another may represent Victory, with a laurel wreath on her head and palm branches in each hand. Other figures (fig. 52) seem to represent warriors; an Amazon with bow and arrow, a swordsman with raised shield attacking an enemy, and two others in one corner fighting a duel. One figure seems to represent a woman rather out of character in that heroic company, as she wears a dress strangely like those of the period of the Revolution. Another may be intended for Diana, while Jupiter, in a striped garment, holds thunderbolts in both hands. These figures are colored black, white, and gray on a buff background like the wall above. This decorative scheme, minus the emblems, is practically identical with the one in the Jaynes house at East Setauket, Long Island.

Both have circular figures of intertwining leaves and vines with roses at the points where they join, arranged vertically, with a narrow border of the same motif—the looped-up drapery of the frieze in the Jaynes room being the only real difference except the change of the colors. The room in Bernardston, while showing a different design, has a frieze with drapery looped up with cords and tassels, which bears a strong resemblance to the frieze in the Jaynes house.

As decorations and studies in harmonious coloring, taking them at their best, it is difficult to find their superior in our modern home decoration, while their strange, piquant quaintness, which belongs so wholly to a past generation, gives them a charm impossible to resist. This forgotten artist had a genius for decoration.

JAYNES HOUSE[1]

THE Jaynes homestead at East Setauket, Long Island, supposed to have been built about 1690, is a fine old specimen of colonial farmhouse, in one room of which, the "East" or "Best Room," the walls are covered with well-preserved frescoes, quite different in design from the others, with the exception of the room at Bernardston, Massachusetts, which it resembles in the design of the frieze, each having looped-up drapery, cords, and tassels.

The frescoes were discovered, as many others have been, under several coats of wall paper. They were painted free-hand in oil on a background of greenish blue, giving a wonderfully soft tone, through which shows a coat of red paint, where the ground color has chipped off. Around the doors and windows is a border suggestive of the design seen on old decorated tin tea trays, while around the top of the room is a wider border of festoons and tassels, now brown with age, very quaint and interesting. The main panels on the walls are filled with crossed sprays giving the suggestion

[1] Photographs by courtesy of Howard C. Sherwood, New York City.

of a series of wreaths, with bottle-green leaves, and orange-red roses at the points of intersection.

The dado is of plaster, separated from the upper section of the wall by a chair rail, painted a greenish blue without any decoration, and since painted over to match the trim. As colors change with age, and the effect of light, this may have been originally

54. PANEL OVER THE FIREPLACE IN THE "EAST ROOM" OF
THE JAYNES HOUSE

a pure blue; the roses also may have been a pure red, although the same yellowing effect of time has changed the color to a very beautiful shade of orange-red.

The frequent monotony of a wide wall surface is overcome by the various panels (fig. 53), each surrounded by a border of leaves and flowers, and the wide, scalloped frieze at the top, with its festoon of drapery, beads, and tassels.

The panel over the fireplace (fig. 54) has a spray of leaves at the center with looped vines on each side, that on the right being abbreviated because the artist, through a miscalculation, did not have sufficient space left for full figures on that side. The panel on the left of the fireplace shows a complete section of the design, with the circular figures formed by crossing the vines placed vertically, and a rose like a bow-knot at points of intersection. The frieze and leaf border combined nearly cover the space around the door. Between two windows (fig. 55) there is a plain section of the wall surrounded by a border and covered by a mirror. Beneath this panel a smaller one fills the space between it and the painted dado with the tops of a pair of sprays with a rose suspended between them, surrounded by the usual border. This small panel, with its soft coloring, has been compared to an old faded Japanese print.

The recent removal of wall paper from an upper room has brought to light similar designs (fig. 56) upon the walls, painted likewise with oil colors. The motif is a leafy vine arranged vertically in graceful curves which almost describe a figure 8, with a rose above and below, the design ending with a half scroll at each end. This design is similar to the one in the other room, but is more graceful, is executed with more dash and vigor, and shows greater skill. It lacks, however, some of the brightness as well as delicacy and charm of color, the soft tones of which make the other room so interesting.

The design is arranged in panels outlined by a frieze at the top and a narrow border around the other three sides, composed of a serpentine vine and leaves. The color of the background varies from a light bluish gray or battleship gray in some panels to a fairly pronounced blue in others, on which the design is painted in tones of reddish brown with traces of yellow here and there and touches of white on the high lights.

The roses are white, shaded with umber or rich brown, with here and there faint traces of pink. The border has a background which now resembles dusty, yellowish olive, darker than the panel, the design being in white shaded with lines of dark brown on the vine and dabs of the same color on the leaves.

Between two windows, corresponding with the one below, there is a small horizontal panel (fig. 57) with the border and S scroll

55. PANELS BETWEEN THE WINDOWS IN THE "EAST ROOM" OF THE JAYNES HOUSE

56. PANELS IN AN UPPER ROOM OF THE JAYNES HOUSE

57. PANEL BETWEEN TWO WINDOWS IN AN UPPER ROOM
OF THE JAYNES HOUSE

figure of the large design, with rosebuds at the center and a lily at the end of the vine; and between the door and the corner of the room, and over the lintel, the space is covered by another elongated scroll and rose figure with the usual border.

This, as a whole, is a very pleasing design, which is much more distinct in figure as well as sharper in outline than the one below, but it is more conventionalized, and the perfect curve of the stem of the vine, together with the short, stiff, scroll leaves, many of which seem to be detached from the vine, have some resemblance to stencil work, the figures being much more like those in the Red House than the wilder, freer, more exuberant design in the lower room.

Judging by the number of stars in the national emblem in the frescoes, the room in the Red House must have been painted first, and as that design of a looped vine occurs again only in the Jaynes house, the latter was evidently done very soon afterward, toward the end of the century, after the British forces left Long Island and New York, for one may assume that not until the country had once more become normal, and some degree of prosperity had returned, would anyone have been justified in having his house so elaborately decorated.

WAID-TINKER HOUSE

THE most ornate of these tapestry frescoes, a veritable bower of flowers, covers the walls of the parlor of the Waid-Tinker House in Old Lyme, Connecticut. It is executed in oils, the dominant tone being a bluish green gray, which passes from soft minor shades to deep, rich tones, relieved by soft shades of buff and red, producing an unusually rich effect. The gray of the background has the soft, illusive quality of moonlight.

The room is about fifteen feet square by eight feet high and for one of its size is very attractive in appearance, due to an ornate chimney-piece with mantel, frieze with dentils, a long, narrow picture panel within a molding with croisetted corners, and scrolled end ornaments. Around the room extends a deep molded cornice with dentils, which in the outside corner rests upon an unusual feature in the form of an engaged square column with fluted sides between dado and capital.

The unit of design (fig. 58), which is repeated in three horizontal rows above the dado, is composed of an oval outlined figure with a drooping leaf on each side, and encloses a cluster of red berries which resemble elongated strawberries. On each side of this figure is another cluster not enclosed, connected with the first or central figure by a festoon of leaves and flowers. A cord and tassel at the center of each festoon, together with the very straight lines above and below, form a small rectangular outline. Each section of wall is surrounded by a narrow border of leaves and flowers, with a frieze of pale buff, on which are deep-toned leaves and roses outlined in red. The frieze is also divided into short sections by a cord and tassel, repeating the small unit of design.

The dado is notable, as a close copy of the dower chest design. It is composed of a

59. FRESCO OF HERALDIC DESIGN (LIONS) IN THE PARLOR OF THE WAID-TINKER HOUSE

58. FRESCO IN THE PARLOR OF THE WAID-TINKER HOUSE, OLD LYME, CONNECTICUT

succession of dark gray arches supported by columns or pilasters of the same color, striped with lines or dashes of red and deep greenish blue as if to represent variegated marble. The fantastic capitals, covered with hair-line scroll figures (which may repre-

60. FRESCO OF HERALDIC DESIGN (EAGLE) IN THE PARLOR OF THE WAID-TINKER HOUSE

sent acanthus leaves) together with the upper section of the column, extend across the face of the arcade to the top. On the light gray background of the intervening panels are painted clusters of flowers on bending stalks, one of large red fuchsias alternating with another variety of flower.

Opposite the door on the left side of the room (fig. 59) two red lions, balanced precariously on a canopy upheld by enormous birds, face each other in the attitude of

61. "AMEN STREET." OVER-MANTEL PANEL IN THE PARLOR OF THE WAID-TINKER HOUSE

heraldic supporters. The escutcheon they uphold has been painted out, but the name *Waid* remains.

On the opposite wall, within a border of three circles, there is a large gray eagle with spread wings (fig. 60), on its breast a shield of seventeen red and gray-white vertical stripes, in its claws an olive branch and arrows. On a ribbon above the shield is the name Weston Brockway. Encircling its head are sixteen small six-pointed stars, which, with the tassels of the frieze, show traces of gold. As these sixteen stars seem to indicate the number of states which composed the Union when the room was painted and as the sixteenth state was Tennessee, admitted in 1796, this room may have been painted sometime between that year and 1803, when the seventeenth state joined the Union.

It is possible that the fact of seventeen stripes on the shield places the room at a later date (1803-1812), but as the same error occurs on the shield on the ceiling of Congress Hall, the number of stripes may have no significance.

An examination of the details suggests the probable use of stencils or patterns on which the design had been sketched, then pricked, for the transfer of the outlines to the wall by means of a pounce filled with white powder, the various parts then being filled in by hand. The intricacy of

62. FLORAL PANEL IN THE WAID-TINKER HOUSE

the design and the endless repetition of certain small figures clearly show the improbability of such a decoration having been painted entirely free-hand over so large a surface.

The narrow, even, scalloped border of dots which outlines each section, could hardly have been painted one at a time free-hand, although the irregular line just under the dots probably was. Each one of the rectangular divisions is so exactly spaced between the straight lines which surround it, and is so accurately repeated, that there is little room for doubt that it was at least outlined by means of a pricked pattern, although the irregularity in size, number, and position of the red berries, which vary from nine to twelve each, and the shape of the leaves and flowers, the shadings of veins and stems, all denote free-hand work.

The serpentine border and the arches and columns in the dado are likewise too evenly spaced, the outlines too even and sharp for free-hand work, although the flower figures at the center of each panel show all the life, vigor, and irregularity of this method, thus giving these frescoes a decided individuality.

The fantastic landscape on the over-mantel panel (fig. 61), known as Amen Street, probably represents a New England village of the period. It is painted in gray tones, the stiff, square white buildings being enlivened with touches of pale red, green, and drab, with red or brown roofs, while in the foreground is an elaborate fence with high gateways, all in white. There seems to be little or no sky, as a waving line of stone wall or bushes with trees and an occasional house reaches to the top of the picture. Several people of tiny proportions are seen walking along the street in the center,

63. FLORAL PANEL BETWEEN THE WINDOWS IN THE WAID-TINKER HOUSE

dressed in the style of the last quarter of the eighteenth century; one of them is a wild roisterer, for he flourishes his wig in one hand and a bottle in the other, as he staggers drunkenly along.

Among the names painted on the buildings are Jin Shop, and S L Inn, and near the latter is a tall pole from which swings the tavern sign. From a tree in the foreground waves a pennant which bears a black eagle so like the one in the Red House that it probably was painted by the same artist. On a building near by is written the name Amen St., which gives the panel its name.

64. FRESCO IN THE PARLOR OF THE H. W. GRAY HOUSE, OLD LYME,
CONNECTICUT

In the room across the hall the same greenish gray tones are seen, but here the wall is undecorated save for a frieze (fig. 62) of leaves and flowers in a double row and a narrow band of the same character, around the other three sides of a large panel, one to each section of the room. Between two windows there is a small panel (fig. 63) treated in the same way, with the addition of a sketch of a vase of flowers and leaves darkly shaded, prominent among them being the fuchsias, hanging from drooping stems.

65. DADO IN THE PARLOR OF THE H. W. GRAY HOUSE

It is supposed that the frescoes in the parlor and hall of the H. W. Gray house were done by the same hand as those in the Tinker house. The walls of the parlor are buff, on which diamond figures are outlined by black beaded lines or cords, with flowers and beads on the points (fig. 64). In these diamonds are alternating horizontal rows of figures, one row consisting entirely of red tulips, the next one composed of turtle doves, blue and white or blue and red in color, each pair being placed face to face. A row of tulips and rosettes at the top forms the frieze.

An important feature of this room is its dado (fig. 65), which has the arched panel design with pilasters extending from base to molding, as in the Tinker house. The arches are red, the pilasters white, the panels buff, and on these last are painted classical or dramatic characters in white with black outlines, which alternate with white evergreen or Christmas trees covered with black stars or needles. One of these figures is a crowned monarch, or Jove with his thunderbolt, sitting on the world; another a cavalier armed with a sword and a shield with a heraldic device; he in turn is followed by a partially draped female figure, on whose extended left hand is poised

66. FRESCO IN THE HALL OF THE H. W. GRAY HOUSE

a black eagle which is, like the others, presumably that of Prussia; while around the corner of the room stands a woman who wears a great hoopskirt and a Gainsborough hat and feather.

The hall design (fig. 66) also consists of diamonds formed by white, threadlike serpentine lines on a pink ground. These diamonds are arranged vertically in sets of

four with the same figure for each set, one having four white hyacinths, another a
ball-like flower outlined in red and blue, while the third contains tulips, red, yellow,
and blue.

Each hyacinth figure has a small red heart at its center and is also enclosed in a
large heart which is outlined in black or white, the whole forming a veritable shrine of
St. Valentine. There is no dado, so the decoration, surrounded by a narrow border of
white loops, extends from floor to ceiling. Although somewhat sketchy in places, and
chalky in appearance, the walls are aglow with warmth and brightness and the figures
are unusual and novel throughout.

67. OVER-MANTEL PANEL IN THE PARLOR OF THE BURROWS HOUSE,
BERNARDSTON, MASSACHUSETTS

BURROWS HOUSE

IN Bernardston, Massachusetts, in the Connecticut River Valley, is an interesting
house built in 1812, and at one time used as a tavern. The parlor or perhaps public
room was frescoed, it is said, by a wandering artist who was supposed to have
been a spy or a deserter from the British army, and, spending the winter of 1813 in
the town, painted the frescoes for his board. One day some men in uniform came and
took him away. He was never heard of again.

This room has become famous throughout the countryside for the beauty and
quaintness of its designs.

Over the mantel (fig. 67) a very strange landscape is seen executed in bluish gray
tones, background, sky, hedges, and water, relieved only by the subdued spots of color
on the fantastic houses placed in two rows on the left, some of which are red, others
white or yellow. The houses are high and narrow with gables of different shapes,
some being semicircular with a cupola; others truncated with slanting sides, very much
like the picturesque houses of Holland. On the street or terrace below are two other
buildings, one looking like two connected white towers, to which are attached a row of
open sheds with pointed roofs. They are slanting to one side as if they had started on
a slow journey downhill, or, becoming tired with the cares of life, were leaning against
the large building at the end, which is partly obliterated.

Beneath the buildings is a light gray field, across the front of which is painted a row of trees with dark tops elongated horizontally, in such a fashion as to give the illusion of a row of large white sheep with black faces standing in a row facing the harbor, looking as if startled into immobility by the approach of the ships. Along the water front near the houses there is a row of trees or bushes with rounded tops resembling balloons of various sizes and shapes, varying from very small ones in the

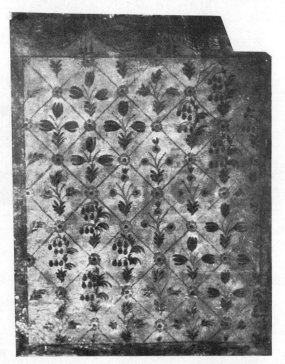

68. PANEL IN THE PARLOR OF THE BURROWS HOUSE

foreground to large ones at the center of the row, intended possibly as examples of topiary art. On the gray water of the harbor are three sailing vessels, their bows pointed toward the town which is so near them that it seems they must go aground before they can change their course. In the distance, above the houses, are several men walking along a highway shaded by trees, some of which are as slender as poplars, while others resemble palms. From the opposite end of the road a coach and four, preceded by a man on horseback, is approaching the town. Below the coach is another road or hedgerow and another row of trees.

It is a quaint, fascinating picture and forcibly reminds one of a very old piece of faded tapestry or arras.

The other wall spaces in the room are covered with rather intricate designs of fruit and flowers (fig. 68) on a light buff background, arranged by diagonal lines into series of diamonds, each one being composed of four smaller ones. Each set of four has the same design. Some have red strawberries with green leaves, which hang in rows of three, two, and three, pendent from slender stems bent into semicircles. Another set has three flowers with red centers looking like partially opened tulips. Another group is composed of small round flowers like daisies with a dark center. On each corner of the small diamonds is another small flowerlike figure. The variations of the figures in corresponding sets in outline, size, and position, although otherwise alike, show that these designs must have been painted at least partially free-hand. At the top of the wall is a frieze of dark looped drapery, held in position by three cords with tassels.

The other three sides of each wall panel are surrounded by a narrow border of similar character.

The dado beneath is divided into many small niches by a dark-colored arcade, in each one of which is a tree, bending to the right as if swept by a strong wind, like those in the landscape over the mantel.

Beneath two of the windows there is a narrow panel of similar design, with scroll figures and flowers minus the diamonds, all in the same colors.

The designs are skillfully drawn, even to minute details, show a fine sense of color values and harmonies, and make a most pleasing and brilliant effect, heightened by a coat of varnish which was applied a few years ago. The difference in effect between these panels and the dull, unvarnished, cold, blue-gray landscape, is startling.

Years ago these frescoes were dark and dingy with dirt and smoke. The present owner restored them to their original beauty by cleaning them by hand with pieces of common bread dough, kneaded into small loaves, which were then carefully rolled over the painted surface. The dough came from the wall perfectly black. This process was continued over every inch of surface, until it was once more fresh and bright.

MATHER HOUSE

IT is said that there is a room in a New Hampshire house which has a dado on which fish are painted in natural colors, some of them measuring two feet or more in length.

In another house, since destroyed, the walls were painted with a series of small scenes like vignettes, placed at regular intervals, each in a frame of scrolls or filigree; while in still another appeared scenes with stiff little pointed trees, with birds much too large for the branches on which they perched, all in painfully strong colors.

There was, until recently covered with wall paper or paint, a room in South Windham, Vermont, frescoed with strange forest scenes in which serpents formed a very prominent part, attracting immediate attention and holding one's gaze fascinated with horror. It may have been the coiled monsters which unintentionally caused the story, but the neighbors say the room was painted by a wandering sailor who demanded a quart of rum a day besides his pay, and that the strange scenes were the result of a prolonged debauch.

The Coolidge house in Plymouth and the Mather house in Marlboro, therefore, seem to be the only ones in Vermont in which old frescoes are preserved today; and the Marlboro house is unique not only because of the number of rooms frescoed in one house, but for the reason that the lower floor is covered with crude, fantastic landscapes, while the rooms above are decorated with skill of a high order, having conventional designs only, in soft, harmonious colors.

The house was built by Captain Dan Mather about 1820. It is a large two-story building with a central hall and two rooms at each side. Near the house were a gristmill, wool-carding mill, fulling mill, starch factory, tannery, boot and shoe shop, and sawmill,—all run by water supplied by the Marlboro South Pond.

Tradition says that the painting of the frescoes on the several rooms and halls was a secret, no one being allowed to see the painter while at work. The scenes in the two halls and parlor are crude in drawing, perspective, and colors. They were painted in water color, free-hand, without any background except that furnished by the white plaster. Tall trees with slender trunks and drooping branches (fig. 69) make the hall resemble an aisle in a forest, with distant views of rolling hills, in natural colors. The principal scene (fig. 70) covers the entire space on the right and through its very crudity is most amusing. Between trees standing like sentinels is a very straight road formed by green and yellow stripes, with large square houses merely outlined in dark green on either side. At first glance the road seems to extend up a very high, steep hill, as if, like Jacob's ladder, it tried to reach to heaven. On closer examination, however,

69. FRESCO IN THE HALL OF THE MATHER HOUSE, MARLBORO, VERMONT

70. FRESCO, VILLAGE SCENE IN THE HALL OF THE MATHER HOUSE

this proves to be an almost childish attempt at perspective. As all the housetops can be seen, possibly the artist expected the observer to imagine himself in a treetop, looking down on the street. To left and right are cultivated fields. This scene may have meant to portray a characteristic tree-shaded street and common of the typical New England village. One huge tree, beginning on the staircase in the lower hall (fig. 71), extends to the ceiling above, while a forest of smaller, similar ones covers the entire wall space of the upper hall.

The parlor was also decorated in the same free crude manner. Over the mantel is a forest scene with green trees set in regular rows, but beneath the landscape and just over the mantel was added, at a later period, in dark bronze-brown, a basket of grapes and other fruit, with leaves and delicate vines and tendrils which extend down each side of the fireplace. The delicate waving hair lines which form the leaves and flowers on the sides are well drawn and look as if they had been executed with a huge pen, like the chairbacks of Hitchcock design. The frieze of the mantel and the fireboard beneath are similarly ornamented in yellow and light and dark brown. In this room is another amusing scene (fig. 72), much like the one in the hall. Here also is a road which seems to go uphill, but in reality is supposed to extend across the level fields. A branch of

71. FRESCO ON THE STAIRCASE IN THE LOWER HALL OF
THE MATHER HOUSE

72. FRESCO IN THE PARLOR OF THE MATHER HOUSE

the road winds and twists across the foreground. Beside it are several houses in out-line only, while in the middle distance is a serpentine road, which is the scene of a lively rabbit hunt. On close examination can be seen first a tawny rabbit closely pur-sued by a hound, then another rabbit closely following the hound, which in its turn is closely pursued by a second hound, in a never-ending race across the landscape.

The color and details of the trees as well as the artist's habit of painting without a background, as seen here, closely resemble the colors and methods employed in Groton, Massachusetts, indicating both as the work of the same artist, although part of the work may have been done by an un-skilled assistant. Possibly, also, the crude details may have been filled in by a member of the owner's family, as they seem very childish.

On the upper floor are three rooms which prove a most agreeable surprise. They are frescoed in tempera, partly free-hand, partly with the use of sten-cils, by a master hand, with designs of fruit, flowers, vines, and leaves in two colors on a light background. The de-signs must have been laid on with great care, a set for each room, and each with a different and decorative chimney-piece, having the same figures as those on the walls but with a more elaborate arrangement.

73. OVER-MANTEL DESIGN IN AN UPPER CHAMBER OF THE MATHER HOUSE

One of the chambers has a most at-tractive over-mantel design (fig. 73) painted on a light buff ground. This space, which is nearly square, is divided into three vertical panels by bands of small, graceful figures resembling curling tendrils. The outside rows extend to the floor, with a second one on the right of the fireplace opening, the space being wider than on the opposite side. At the top of the two outside panels are the figures of a horse and rider in silhouette, while below is a starlike ornament of nine long, narrow leaves. At the bottom of each panel, and just over the mantel, there is a basket composed of dots of dark color, filled with five graceful curving stems with leaves and a round red berry at the end of each. Between these baskets and the mantel is another border composed of a serpentine vine with leaves and flowers. Another border of semicircles and dots is seen over each door, while around the room extends a wide frieze of semicircles with an indented edge above a double row of small dashes, with six-pointed leaflike figures and dotted circles beneath each. These narrow panels, about a foot wide, also extend around the room from floor to ceiling, the large leaf figure alternating diagonally as well as vertically with a star of four large and eight small points with a similar center. At the foot of the wall near the floor another figure is used in the narrow border of circles of five horizontal lines or zones, separated from each other by four dots. These figures of dots, semicircles, and stars closely resemble the figures seen in the Cromwell, Connecticut, house.

A room on the opposite side of the hall has a soft, pale rose-pink ground similarly divided into vertical panels by bands of small diamond-shaped figures, formed by

74. PANEL IN AN UPPER CHAMBER OF THE MATHER
HOUSE

four vertical lines with leaves between. On these panels (fig. 74) the alternating figures have in one instance five leaves, in another a star of six pointed rays and six red berries within a dotted circle. The frieze also differs, being a composition of interlacing lines combined with a leaf motive, forming a succession of connecting ovals heavily shaded on one side.

At the bottom of the wall there is a wavy vine and leaf border in light green. The round berries or dots have a deep red color, the other figures being soft green or greenish yellow.

The over-mantel design in this room (fig. 75) has only two panels, as it is narrower. Here the same figures are repeated, with the basket of flowers.

A rear room likewise has a delicate pink background, with vertical panels as in the other rooms, but with another set of figures with a dot and leaf motive, a large five-leaf figure in yellow with an alternate figure of four deep red berries, with circles and wedges.

75. OVER-MANTEL DESIGN IN AN UPPER CHAMBER OF
THE MATHER HOUSE

Over the mantel is repeated the basket of flowers or berries, the one figure common to all, one to each of the three panels, with the leaf and flower border of the first room.

The frieze of this room is a serpentine vine with dots and dashes representing leaves and starlike flowers, a single row of dots against the ceiling, a double row at the base of the frieze.

The design is finished at the bottom of the wall with the frieze of semicircles and dots which is also at the top of the first room. Throughout these rooms there is a pleasing variety of figures and colors, the latter soft, harmonious, and unobtrusive. Where the wall space at the side of the fireplace is narrow, there is only one border, which is a continuation from the ceiling; but where the space is wider, there is a repetition next the mantel, thereby avoiding overcrowding a narrow space, and properly filling a wide one.

Eighteen or more different figures can be counted in these rooms, and as there are two colors for most if not all of them, a very large number of stencils must have been used to make the different parts of some two hundred figures.

The colors, where not damaged, are clear, bright, and fresh in appearance even after the lapse and wear of generations. This is stencil work of a high order, and forms a valuable collection of designs, which could be used to advantage today.

COOLIDGE HOUSE[1]

TOWARD the close of the Revolution, John Coolidge, the great-great-grandfather of the President, following the Ticonderoga trail, settled in what is now the town of Plymouth, Vermont, where he built a log cabin in 1781. Here he prospered, and later built the first frame house in the town, about 1820.

Each room in the house, with the exception of the kitchen, was frescoed in tempera

[1] By courtesy of Mr. Walter Gilman Page of Boston, president Massachusetts Art League, who discovered the house during the summer of 1924.

76. FRAGMENTS FROM THE COOLIDGE HOUSE,
PLYMOUTH, VERMONT

*Courtesy of the Massachusetts Historical Society, Boston,
Masachusetts.*

77. STENCIL DESIGN IN THE PARLOR OF THE COOLIDGE HOUSE

78. STENCIL DESIGN IN THE PARLOR BEDROOM OF THE
COOLIDGE HOUSE

79. STENCIL DESIGN IN THE GUEST CHAMBER OF THE COOLIDGE
HOUSE

on the plaster, with designs similar to those in the Marlboro house, and shows the same excellence of work and design, the well-drawn figures being clear and sharp, the colors pleasing.

Several fragments (fig. 76) of the painted plaster which had fallen from the walls are now in the rooms of the Massachusetts Historical Society in Boston. One has a light, soft green leaf figure which resembles a fleur-de-lis on a cream-colored background. Another fragment with a buff ground has a deep red lotus with a green sepal, a long curved green stem and leaf which alternates with the oak leaf in the parlor (fig. 77) with a border at base of wall and dado. On either side of this design was painted a vertical stripe which divided the wall into narrow panels. This stripe consists of a succession of two short curved figures in green which resemble bent-over papyrus buds with a small red heart between each pair.

On the third fragment with a pale pink ground is a much larger flower figure with curving green petals well open as if in full bloom, just beneath which is a red heart.

The parlor bedroom walls (fig. 78) are also divided into narrow vertical panels of lines and dashes, and have flower and geometrical figures alternating. The wall is finished at the top with an outlined festooned frieze with cords and tassels.

The design in the front hall is very dim owing to extreme exposure to the weather at all seasons. The interesting portion which is left includes a spread eagle around which are many stars, although the exact number is uncertain.

The best-preserved and most elaborate frescoes (fig. 79) in the house are in a corner of the guest chamber. The lotus is repeated here with a different oak leaf figure arranged also in vertical panels by narrow stripes of lines and dots. The foot of the wall has a border of circular figures and oak leaves and dotted lines. The wall design also appears in the dado, which ends with another geometrical border of figures of a different character. The designs in this corner produce a mosaic effect of great artistic merit as if inlaid instead of being painted.

HUBBARD HOUSE

A MOST unusual form of wall painting for a private residence is seen in the Hubbard house, for the decoration consists of Masonic emblems. In one room (fig. 80) over the fireplace is the square and compass with a G at the center, and beneath it a large urn with long drooping leaves and what resemble cherries hanging from slender stems, painted in water colors on the plaster. The compass is a deep, rich blue, while all the other objects are a vivid green, on a white background.

On the opposite side of the house, in what was called the ballroom, the wall decorations were quite different in character. The illustration (fig. 81) shows a small section at one side of and beneath a window. This consists of a vertical panel from dado to ceiling, with three weeping willow trees separated by two large, eight-pointed stars. A narrow border on each side is formed of alternate crescents and stars, said to be devices in the Hubbard coat-of-arms. Above is a section of frieze consisting of a large semicircle which springs from a horizontal line and encloses the double star and a

80. OVER-MANTEL PANEL IN THE HUBBARD
HOUSE, CROMWELL, CONNECTICUT

figure which resembles a lighted candle on each side, a star forming the flame. Outside the circle and just over each one of the narrow borders is the same candlelike figure, with a star above it, in this case larger than the others.

Beneath the panel, extending horizontally around the lower part of the room, is another border, in green and black. This is wider, and consists of a series of slender arched figures, each with a cross in the center. On the left, beyond the palm tree just under the window, is a vertical wavy vine with small leaves.

The house, a substantial two-story structure on the Hartford Turnpike, was built in 1794, and was maintained as a tavern from 1808 to 1833. Local tradition states that the Masons of Cromwell, then known as Upper Middletown, met here because of some disagreement with their brethren of Middletown, to whose lodge they belonged. It is quite possible that the use of this out-of-the-way tavern was the result of the anti-Masonic agitation of 1826-1827, which would establish an approximate date for the frescoes. The name of the painter, who is said to have come from Hartford or New Haven, is long since forgotten.

GRANT HOUSE

THE Grant homestead of North Saco, Maine, while geographically isolated, is included in the Connecticut River Valley group because the similarity of design and treatment of its frescoes indicate that the design, and possibly the execution, were by the painter who decorated some of these other houses.

It is excellent stencil work, and is seen in the hall and one room. The hall has been papered, but one corner of it shows in pale green the oak leaf design of the Mather house in Marlboro, Vermont. The room, while different in other respects, has two similar borders and stripes in brown (fig. 82) and the woven flower basket (fig. 83) with slender stalks, tulips, and buds in red and green, four of which are placed over the mantel in a row. On the two center baskets are poised red birds with black wings, a feature peculiar to the room. The other figures are an orange sunflower with dark brown center; a maple leaf within a wreath of smaller leaves; a geometric figure, and a large leaf border around the upper wall in black and orange, the background of the room being a dull gray. This room adds several new stencil figures to those seen in the other houses by this artist.

81. FRESCO IN THE BALLROOM OF THE
HUBBARD HOUSE

82. STENCIL DESIGN IN THE GRANT HOUSE,
SACO, MAINE

83. STENCIL DESIGN SHOWING BASKETS AND BIRDS IN THE GRANT HOUSE

This flower basket design is probably similar to the one formerly in the Stebbins house in Deerfield, Massachusetts, and was perhaps the work of the same artist.

DEERFIELD, MASSACHUSETTS

FORMERLY there were several good examples of frescoes in the town, some belonging to the stencil group and others to the later landscape group, but unfortunately only two examples remain. One is in a room in the Arms house. The design (fig. 84) is a spray of three round red flowers with bluish green leaves and stems in a diamond figure, arranged in oblique rows with a rosette at each intersection, on a light buff ground, each section of wall above the white wood dado having a narrow border of black wavy lines, similar to the other houses of the Connecticut River Valley group, and closely resembling the design in the hall of the Gray house in Lyme. The design is carried around the door with a narrow panel effect, the figures being spiral stems with flowers which shade from blue to red; and it is noticeable that these circular figures are very like those in the upper room of the Jaynes house.

84. STENCIL DESIGN IN THE ARMS HOUSE, DEERFIELD, MASSACHUSETTS

Around the room there is the usual festooned frieze with three red cords hanging at regular intervals. Over the mantel there is a Boston Harbor scene, blackened and nearly defaced, but showing the characteristics of the one in Bernardston.

The room across the hall is also frescoed, the design being a looped or spiral leaf and stem figure almost black in color, with a similar border around the edge painted on a light terra cotta ground. The walls of this room are temporarily covered with paper.

The other remaining example (fig. 85) is in the small entry of the Frary house. Part of the plaster had to be removed but the design was carefully completed by Mrs. Madeline Wynne. This wall shows a spiral figure with tulips, forget-me-nots, and others, with leaves and long slender stems, on a pinkish buff ground.

In Memorial Hall there is a large wood panel (fig. 86) which was taken from the old Burk tavern in Bernardston, a few miles away. The picture is almost a duplication of the harbor scene in the Burrows house, but on a larger scale. It is now dark and dingy, but its principal features are easily distinguished. There are the same ships in the foreground, with white sails, red houses on the left much more American in character than in the other picture, the highway in the

85. FRESCO IN THE ENTRY OF THE FRARY HOUSE, DEERFIELD, MASSACHUSETTS

background with the same curious trees, the coach, and men walking. Nobody knows the name of the artist, but there is a persistent tradition in Deerfield, as in Bernardston, that he was a British spy, who, during the War of 1812, while working for his board in these various taverns and houses, overheard the news and gossip of the country-side and transmitted it to the enemy until, suspected of spying, he was arrested and taken away.

There is also a fireboard from the Ryther house in Bernardston (fig. 87) with an attractive design on a mottled greenish gray background, its freedom and boldness making it very decorative. The design is a large bouquet of red flowers which with the sprays of leaves and stems are outlined with green. It stands in a little white and pink vase, the whole framed by a black band and an outer border in imitation of red bricks. It so closely resembles the bouquet of fuchsias in the Tinker house in Lyme that it might be ascribed to the same artist, although the local tradition credits it to the spy who painted the harbor scenes.

86. HARBOR SCENE. PANEL FROM THE BURK TAVERN, BERNARDSTON, MASSACHUSETTS

The most interesting frescoes in Deerfield, however, seem to have been in the old Saxton tavern, but unfortunately they became so defaced that it was necessary to cover them over. They are described by Miss Margaret C. Whiting[1] of Deerfield, as follows:

"Each space on the cramped stairway, which is composed of three sets of narrow steps with two landings, is filled by a landscape, whose features were chosen to adequately fill its boundaries; there is about it something reminiscent of the double page of 'natural wonders,' in the front of the old geography, it is true, yet it is done in a manner that makes a serious claim on our praise. Note the really lovely drawings of the hanging, leafy sprays of a water plant which swings downward from a crag against the cataract; study the varied and thoughtfully introduced weeds and rushes growing along the pool below,—these have a fidelity of observation, worthy of our recognition. . . .

"Each part of the wall bears its own landscape theme, . . . but the side-wall of the stairway is treated as a single composition the interest centering in a large water-

[1] Margaret C. Whiting, "Old-time Mural and Floor Decorations in Deerfield and Vicinity," in *History and Proceedings of the Pocumtuck Valley Memorial Association*, Volume VI.

fall, which descends, from a dark, towering rock at the top, between bold, confining cliffs, and, with a wide spread of broken water and surf, dashes away under a shelving, rocky foreground, where a stag stoops its antlered head to drink, just above the base-boards at the bottom. On the curving surface of the wall over the stairs, forest trees and rocks are seen, and the taller wall at the head of the flight of steps corresponds in character to the wild and rugged features of the whole. The panels on either side of

87. FIREBOARD FROM THE RYTHER HOUSE, BERNARDSTON, MASSACHUSETTS

the front window which lights the narrow upper hall, have gentler themes, in lake views, with distant mountains; on the bank of one a fisherman may dimly be seen under a willow tree, while a cottage is discernible in the foreground of the other. Beneath the window is a lengthwise pattern, which would now be called a 'dado,' composed of big looped garlands of carefully drawn palm branches, with red roses or pomegranates in the middle of each. Altogether, an ambitious conception, vigorously carried out in colors which once must have shown a considerable variety of blues and olive browns and dull greens, ochres and russet.''

Miss Whiting mentions two other instances of painted walls now obscured by paper. In the Allen house, ''a landscape form of decoration, in a design of large trees and mountains and meadows, done in browns and greens.'' And in the house built by Asa Stebbins in 1799, ''a design quite different in character from the others. . . . It had a chintz-like pattern arranged in an effect of stripes, the figures being an urn holding three stiff little tulips and a floral sprig of an unknown botanical connection, placed alternately, one above another, about a foot apart; this was repeated all about the rooms. The top of the wall was finished by a border of looped garlands of leaves, and the windows and doors were outlined by a leafy band. In curious contrast to the vivacious look of this pattern was the introduction of a picture enclosed in an oval line, that was painted over the mantel; this was a landscape, but . . . undecipherable.''

It is interesting to compare the description of this design with those in Marlboro and North Saco.

PORTER HOUSE

A CHARMING stencil design was found by Mr. J. Frederick Kelly of New Haven a short time ago in the old Porter house in South Coventry, Connecticut.

It represents baskets and scrolls in green and flowers in red, which were painted on the plaster in tempera but without any background. The separations between the sections of the figures are characteristic of stencil work with exceptions here and there which indicate free-hand work. Evidently the designs were transferred to the wall by means of a pricked pattern, stenciled, and finished by hand.

In one room is a frieze which consists of round light red roses with pale green leaves and stems, an occasional flower or leaf being nearly obliterated through the effects of time, rough usage, and a covering of wall paper. The rose design is about eight inches high and alternates with another of rosebuds and leaves.

On the panel over the fireplace was painted a very decorative green flower pot with a rose bush in the same colors, and a cluster of red roses.

In another room a serpentine vertical border of red and green leaves divides the wall into narrow panels from floor to frieze. This frieze is unusually light and fanciful. It consists of festoons of small red and green leaves in alternation, with pendent figures between the sections as well as in the space at the center. One has a star figure above a circle of triangles; another is more conventional with heavy bars at its base, while a third is composed of a circle of eight small flowers like a rosette.

Another motif is a green weeping willow tree, its branches bending down to the ground. This tree corresponds closely with those in the house in Cromwell and may have been by the same artist, which would place them in the period from 1808 to 1830.

FOREST FARM

O N the New Boston road, about ten miles above Winsted, Connecticut, stands a country house now known as ''Forest Farm,'' built about one hundred and twenty years ago by one Beldens. A room in this house has the charm of the unexpected, which is one of the attributes of these old frescoes. Although originally all the rooms in the house were frescoed with stenciled designs on the plaster, this upper room only was retained intact after the removal of the accumulated layers of wall paper.

The designs are stenciled on a grayish white background of rough plaster, and consist of vines which trail upward over the walls at intervals like narrow panels, with circles of set flower designs between them; above is an elaborate frieze. Over the mantel an unusually quaint design covers the chimney-breast. It is composed of vases filled with flowers, and very large birds which perch on the branches of small trees, in a naïve but decorative manner.

96. OVER-MANTEL FRESCO IN THE WINN HOUSE, WAKEFIELD, MASSACHUSETTS
Courtesy of the Boston Photo News Company.

American Landscape Group

THE Landscape Period of 1838 (the last of the old series) comprises a distinctive group of frescoes devoted to American scenery, with local views by men bearing American names, and seems to be confined to New England. As with the first landscapes by the Italian, Cornè, they are panoramic, but bear no other resemblance to his work, for many of them are crude in color and drawing, others only partially finished, some even resembling infantile attempts with brush and pencil. And yet some of the crudest views have certain characteristics, such as the type and color of the trees of the Marlboro house, which connect them with others of a higher degree of workmanship. This series shows no connection with or development from any previous group or set of decorations, and it apparently led to no later advance in this branch of decoration unless it can be found in the work of the painters —decorators who produced the scenes and accessories for the theaters—or in the work of later landscape artists, or others who at that time swarmed over the country. They generally began by painting landscapes, though they frequently abandoned that form of art for portraiture in order to make a living, especially before the landscapes of American scenery by Cole and his followers established their popularity in the estimation of the public.

Although there is but slight connection between the frescoes and the landscapes painted on canvas and framed (each an entity in itself instead of being panoramic), it is at least a coincidence that both made their appearance about the same time. That some of the frescoes may have been the first attempts of artists who later became well known is seen in the experience of Francis Alexander, an artist of the day, who shared with his contemporaries many of the adventures, and frequently pathetic experiences, met with on the road to success.

Alexander was a poor country lad, born in Windham County, Connecticut, in 1800, whose only education was obtained in the district school. At the age of twenty, while a master in the school, he painted a water color of a pickerel, and this excited so much admiration that he at once abandoned farming for sign painting.

After having earned a little money, he went to New York for instruction, but his funds were soon exhausted and he returned to the farm, where he indulged his love of scenery by decorating the plaster walls of a room with rude landscapes enlivened by domestic animals.

Although the scenes excited the wonder of the neighbors as on the previous occasion, the frescoes brought no orders, so he turned to portraiture, which alone seemed to hold any promise of financial success. Several of his portraits of relatives were so admired that his "fame had now spread half a mile in one direction." He then wandered from town to town seeking orders and met with such success as a portrait painter that he won both fame and fortune in later years in Boston, where he established his studio.

How crude those landscapes were cannot now be judged, but they identify him with that form of wall decoration, and give an earlier date (1822) in connection with this group.

As Brooklyn and Canterbury are both in Windham County, in which Alexander lived, it is quite possible that the panel pictures described on pages 15, 16, and 17, were painted by him. Two of these abound with animals, which also occupied a prominent place in the paintings done in Alexander's own home, and the third, a crude harbor scene, may have been inspired by his trip to New York.

Many of the scenes in this group are on too large a scale for the confined space they occupy, and the colors too strong. Some of the landscapes are conventionalized, and many details look as if they had been cut from colored paper and pasted on the wall. Separate scenes or sections also bear a strong resemblance to stage scenery, drop curtains, and set pieces.

Possibly some of these frescoes are the work of men trained in scene painting, and if placed on a well-lighted stage, they might, when seen from a proper focal distance, lose their harshness, and their glaring defects might become lost in the general decorative effect.

In these scenes there is a bewildering collection of many varieties of trees, some of which have an exotic appearance, and many plants and grasses, the elm tree being prominent in Westwood, North Reading, and Wakefield. Other trees, with rounded tops and drooping, plume-like branches of a greenish blue color, which have been compared to those on old Persian pottery, are characteristic of the scenes in Marlboro, Groton, and to a less degree in Winthrop; and small, prim, sharply pointed cedars like exclamation points, appear in Groton and Winthrop. Harbor or river scenes with islands, early steamships, sloops, full-rigged ships, and houses of the beginning of the last century, with white fences enclosing a small plot of land in front of each, are common to nearly every locality.

The color schemes also vary from polychrome with a dominating blue, somber green, or soft gray, to a sepia monotone.

The material used appears to have been of excellent quality, for it does not readily rub off and has a hard smooth surface which takes varnish without injury to colors or design except to make them darker in tone.

The colors are very fresh and bright where not damaged, as if the scenes were painted recently instead of nearly a century ago.

WESTWOOD, MASSACHUSETTS

MORE than twenty houses in the vicinity of Westwood, Dedham, and Dover had one or more rooms frescoed during the late thirties. Most, if not all, of these were evidently painted by the same hand, and as "R. Porter—1838," is on one of the scenes, this was probably the painter's name. Nevertheless, Mrs. Abbie F. Robbins, an elderly resident of Westwood, insists that the artist's name was Swift. She does not remember having seen him, but he was often mentioned during her childhood. According to this report, the painter, who came from a town in eastern Connecticut, worked free-hand and painted very rapidly, often doing a room in two or three days. He used neither diagrams nor drawings, and composed his designs as he went along.

Upon entering the hall of the Colburn house in Westwood one almost stumbles against a great ledge of dark brown rock (fig. 88) which extends up the staircase, its top lost to view in the sky and clouds above. At the top of the highest peak stands a man in the dress of the period, one hand holding a cane, the other the hand of a boy who reluctantly follows. Below them, on various points of rock, are goats which attract the attention of a dog or wolf, watching from a still lower position. A large tree in browns and green divides the scene at the center. Beyond the ledge are mountains and white clouds and blue sky. On one of the rocks is painted the name "R. Porter—1838."

Above the dado on the opposite side of the hall there is a harbor view (fig. 89) with a wooded island in bright natural colors, and square white houses, with hills in the distance. A steamboat of early type, bearing the name of *Victory,* and several other vessels are sailing toward the open sea.

In the foreground is a four-barred fence. At the center of the scene stands a large elm tree which, with the ferns and grasses, is characteristic of this group of landscapes.

89. FRESCO IN THE HALL OF THE COLBURN HOUSE

88. FRESCO UP THE STAIRCASE IN THE COLBURN HOUSE, WESTWOOD, MASSACHUSETTS

91. FRESCO OPPOSITE THE HEAD OF THE STAIRS IN THE WEST HOUSE

90. FRESCO IN THE HALL OF THE WEST HOUSE, WESTWOOD, MASSACHUSETTS

The hall of the West house in the same town has its harbor scene and steamboat—this time the *Liberty*—and in the harbor (fig. 90) is a large island with prim white buildings, in the midst of fields of various shades of green, divided into small square plots.

Opposite the head of the stairs (fig. 91) a military officer dressed in a blue coat, yellow breeches, black boots, and cocked hat, is seen riding a red horse.

92. FRESCO IN THE HALL OF THE SUMNER HOUSE, WESTWOOD, MASSACHUSETTS

At the foot of the hall of the old Sumner house, situated in the Clapboardtree district of Westwood, there is painted a lake (fig. 92) with a steamboat and a waterfall, a background of sharp pointed hills, and a large square red house on the left. From this point another steep, gloomy ledge extends up the staircase, and on the crags are seen a deer-hunter and his quarry. Blue and blue-green predominate. There is also a sea view with a square-rigged ship under full sail.

The Baker house in Westwood contains frescoes very similar to the others in the same town. In one section (fig. 93) two horsemen are riding at full speed toward the brink of a rocky cliff, in pursuit of a deer which has just leaped over the edge. In another (fig. 94) stands a large tower on the brow of a steep hill; two cats have been chased up a tree (fig. 95) by a dog; in the corner is a small drawing of a 'cello with the bow laid across the strings.

93, 94, 95. FRESCOES IN THE BAKER HOUSE, WESTWOOD, MASSACHUSETTS

WINN HOUSE AND COLONIAL INN[1]

LANDSCAPES of a similar type (fig. 96) adorn the Winn house in Wakefield, Massachusetts, although it is said that the scenes in this house owe their brown color (for they are in monotone) to the fact that they were done over in 1910, the color only, however, being changed. The principal scene is over the mantel and shows the usual gently sloping hill with the usual houses on the top. In the foreground, at the foot of the hill, are two men wearing tall beaver hats, riding horses at full speed toward a large house on the left with a square yard in front enclosed by a fence. On another side of the room a flock of sheep is quietly grazing, undisturbed by the hurrying horsemen.

In an old house in North Reading, Massachusetts, now known as the Colonial Inn, there are two more rooms of the same general character, one of which (fig. 97) is said to contain a view of Andover Hill, with the buildings of the period. On the left

[1] Photographs by courtesy of G. E. Campbell, Wakefield, Massachusetts.

97. FRESCO IN THE COLONIAL INN, NORTH READING,
MASSACHUSETTS

98. FRESCO IN THE HALL OF THE COLONIAL INN

99. FRESCO IN THE COLONIAL INN

wall of the hall there is a range of hills (fig. 98) beyond a wide river with islands, white houses, great trees, a full-rigged ship and a steamboat, a crew in a rowboat, and on the top of the highest hill a windmill. In the foreground are various types of plants and grasses, which may have been intended to represent ferns and the silver mullen.

One view presents a large town (fig. 99) on the crest of a slope in the distance, small trees set in very regular rows and masses of white clouds, and in the foreground, tall trees and the characteristic plants, all in sepia.

Some of these sepia frescoes have white high lights, which give them the appearance of having been partially covered by a light fall of snow.

Tradition claims that these rooms, like those of the same period in the other towns, were painted by the decorator merely for room and board.

GROTON, MASSACHUSETTS

A SHORT distance outside the town of Groton stands the old Cob (Coburn) Inn, a three-story brick building erected about 1800. It is many years since it ceased to entertain the public, and became a private residence.

Frescoes in color completely cover the walls of the hall which runs through the center of the house, the staircase, the upper hall, and the ballroom, which occupies the whole of the top floor. Modern wall paper has been laid over some parts of the lower hall, but the rest has fortunately been preserved. The subjects comprise houses, trees, fields, low hills, islands, and ships, which gaily extend around the four walls without repetition. The same characteristics of design are seen here as in Westwood, and doubtless were painted by the same artist.

Apparently he began below and worked upward, as the scenes on the first floor are complete, while in the upper room are only sketches partially painted in, with the original plaster for the sky and water, giving a silhouette effect to most of it. Although nearly all of the work is crude there are parts which are very good, with a certain fascination in their decorative effect and historical interest, as many of the frescoes represent local scenes and buildings of the period. It is interesting also because the very incompleteness of the work shows the artist's method. One wonders if this marks the end of his career, or whether the owner's funds gave out before the frescoes could be completed.

The most interesting section of the ballroom is at the end (figs. 100, 101) on the right from the head of the staircase. The roof forms a low arch and between this arch and the dado are two narrow spaces separated by a heavy beam. On the upper section at the left are low hills and fields with a group of houses painted white, red, and yellow, partly hidden by trees. The land is yellow shading into green. Near the center is a large white house surrounded by cedar trees, while a large tree of different character, extending from foreground to skyline, bears a white, red-bordered sign with the name Cob written on it, with figures or letters underneath erased. Near the house can be seen a file of ten soldiers dressed in long white trousers, red coats, and high black hats with upright, red, white-tipped plumes.

The trees have gray trunks outlined in black, a large one at the right being green on the left side and gray on the right, without any apparent reason.

The lower section has islands, tall trees on the shore line which divide it into sections, a full-rigged ship, and the ubiquitous steamboat, black, with a yellow band along

102. OVER-MANTEL FRESCO IN THE BALLROOM OF THE COB INN

the side. The ship is a lead-pencil drawing even to the shading of the sails, with the exception of the hull, which is painted black. As it would be practically impossible to paint in the sky and water after having painted all the rest of the design, it seems as if the artist never intended to do so in this instance.

The over-mantel of one of the fireplaces (fig. 102) has a conical yellow hill, near the top of which stands a red house, which resembles the façade of the old inn with its

100, 101. FRESCOES IN THE BALLROOM OF THE COB INN, GROTON, MASSACHUSETTS

sloping lawn, a row of cedars on the left slope, and two large trees in the foreground, one on each side. In the corner of the wall on the left stand two pert cedar trees, balanced on the right by a group of slender trees which may be birches.

103. FRESCO IN THE PRIEST HOUSE, GROTON, MASSACHUSETTS

At the other end of the town, in Mr. D. L. Priest's house, are similar frescoes by the same artist; the scenes resemble the others but are completely finished. Again it is a harbor scene (fig. 103) with a creamy sky and ocean of a darker shade, with a sloop in the offing, and in the foreground a small boat and a steamer with the name *J. D. Poor* on its paddle-box. Some of the small trees look as if they had been trimmed with shears. At the center is a tree which covers a large part of the scene, its left side green, its trunk and right side colored gray.

NORMAN STREET HOUSE

IN an old house on Norman Street in Salem is another set of frescoes, dating from about 1838 and painted with water color on the walls of a small circular hall. Only a few of many scenes, however, have escaped a thick coating of green paint, which makes a sharp outline around the trees and buildings, and gives one the impression that the scenes were cut from some magazine and pasted on the walls at intervals.

On the upper section (fig. 104) is seen a yellow house with a red wing, and a lawn in front sloping down to water on which a small brown boat is sailing. The water also appears to be the sky for the small scene just below with mountains and blue water and two sailboats. Below this scene one can just distinguish part of a steamboat painted yellow, with a tall funnel from which black smoke is streaming. To the left of the steamboat is a small sailing craft and a large building of unusual shape surrounded by trees. There is also a long line of yellow houses, having red roof lines and chimneys, the most imposing building being a church in the center of the group.

104. FRESCO IN THE CIRCULAR HALL (UPPER SECTION) OF THE NORMAN STREET HOUSE, SALEM, MASSACHUSETTS

On the lower section of the wall (fig. 105) is a two-story dwelling with a veranda and doorway with a fanlight and sidelights, corresponding with those still to be seen in the city. To the left is a stable, while beyond that is an arcade of several arches. Near by is a brown one-horse chaise, with the top up, from which protrude the legs of a man driving a bay horse. Near the entrance of the house is a group of three persons in the quaint costume of the period. The man is dressed in black coat and trousers, and high hat with a rolling brim: the woman in a yellow dress with wide

105. FRESCO IN THE CIRCULAR HALL (LOWER SECTION) OF THE NORMAN
STREET HOUSE

106. FRESCO IN THE HALL OF THE KNOWLTON HOUSE,
WINTHROP, MAINE

107. FRESCO IN THE HANSON HOUSE, WINTHROP, MAINE

sleeves, a bonnet, and red kerchief about her neck. She is holding by the hand a child dressed in dark clothes, a bonnet, and long skirt. Just beyond the house is the national flag, showing thirteen stripes and twenty-four stars. This little hall, with its spiral staircase, probably was originally covered with a complete series of similar scenes and characters winding with the stairs from top to bottom, a kaleidoscope of color.

WINTHROP, MAINE

IN Winthrop, Maine, are three houses in which frescoes have been preserved, all of which have the same characteristics and show the same technique as those in the towns of Westwood, North Reading, and Groton. The hall frescoes in the Knowlton house have a special significance because they bear a signature "E. J. Gilbert" beneath a bow, but without a date. Nevertheless his work so closely resembles

109. OVER-MANTEL FRESCO IN THE HANSON HOUSE

that in the towns mentioned above, that they probably were painted within a few years of 1838.

The dominant color of the hall (fig. 106) is a light, soft gray, all the other colors being in soft minor tones, the tree trunks brown, the leaves of the trees and the fields dull olive green, the house and barns in red. On this section of the hall, which is near the front door, can be seen four distinct varieties of trees, each one of which is picturesque. The square red house with the fanlight over the doorway, the white fence and arched gateway, belong to the early part of the nineteenth century.

Up the stairway, extending to the ceiling above, are great trees, which seem to cast shadows over the hall. Below the landscape is a wide, gray dado, and at its foot, close to the floor, there is a border composed of a serpentine vine with small pointed leaves on each side, in pale green.

The Hanson house in the same town contains a room painted in similar style (figs. 107, 108) with scenes which extend around the walls in a continuous panorama of rolling fields, houses here and there, groups of trees, a river with the usual ship, small boats, and island. Over the mantel (fig. 109) are seen, beyond a screen of trees, high pointed hills on the edge of a wide plain with an occasional house. The light green fields are in strong contrast to the dark, somber trees and the red roofs of the houses.

110. FRESCO IN THE STEVENS HOUSE, WINTHROP, MAINE

108. FRESCO IN THE HANSON HOUSE

The colors are rather dark as a whole, partly due to the effect of the varnish which was recently applied.

The third frescoed room in Winthrop is in the upper story of an old building owned by Mr. Stevens, and used by him as both store and dwelling.

The deep color of the wide expanse of sky and water (fig. 110) gives the room a dominating tone of blue. The general characteristics of the others are seen here, the sea view on one side, however, being much larger, the islands and ships more numerous. The most interesting section is over the fireplace (fig. 111), and this view perhaps

111. OVER-MANTEL FRESCO IN THE STEVENS HOUSE

represents the town as it appeared a hundred years ago. Along what seems to be a street, with a typical New England village green, or common, shaded by tall trees forming green arches overhead, are many square, flat-roofed houses, yellow, red, and white in color. To the right, on the stump of a tree, is an eagle or hawk and in the distance are hills on which are many small umbrella-shaped trees. Along the horizon are great white pointed clouds which give the effect of mountains covered with snow.

The colors in this room, except where damaged by water or abrasion, show their remarkably permanent quality, for they are still fresh and clear.

From an artistic point of view the work in these rooms is crude and sketchy. The trees and bushes especially give the appearance of having been hastily executed, the colors are too strong and the scale too large for the room, but the paintings nevertheless are decorative and quaint.

112. HARBOR SCENE. FRESCO IN THE "PAINTED ROOM" IN "QUILLCOTE,"
HOLLIS, MAINE

"QUILLCOTE"[1] AND THE FURLONG, DALTON, AND SWEET HOUSES

OTHER houses in Maine villages containing frescoes of the same character and period by an unknown artist are "Quillcote" (the home of the late Kate Douglas Wiggin) in Hollis, the Furlong house in Limerick, the Dalton and Sweet houses in North Parsonsfield, and two in Buxton.

"Quillcote" was built in 1823, or soon after, by Jabez Bradbury, who occupied the house until 1835; and as the walls were painted during his occupancy, they antedate those in Westwood by several years. According to tradition, the work was done by a painter from Boston, who mixed his colors with skim milk.

The scenes in the "Painted Room" in "Quillcote," like the others of this group, are panoramic and encircle the room. They show the general characteristics observable in the other rooms of the period, including the prominent fernlike plant in the foreground, peculiar trees, and houses of the early years of the century. Here, too (fig. 112), is the ubiquitous harbor scene with full-rigged ships, sloops, and an island, and

[1] Photographs by courtesy of Miss Nora Archibald Smith.

on the right side a very decorative tree whose drooping branches resemble one on the walls of the Stevens house in Winthrop. The scene over the mantel (fig. 113) carries the resemblance still further by showing a New England village street shaded by a long line of cedar or poplar trees, which nearly hide a row of houses, with jagged mountains in the background. On each side are very tall trees which form an arch overhead. A noticeable feature of this room, because out of character with the land-

113. OVER-MANTEL FRESCO IN THE "PAINTED ROOM" OF "QUILLCOTE"

scapes, is a stenciled frieze composed of bead figures in rows and festoons, which closely resemble those in Cromwell and Marlboro, from which they may have been copied.

The clear, sharp outlines of foliage and other details are in strong contrast to their frequently blurred appearance in other houses of this group, and give them a more natural appearance.

The colors are soft, delicate tones of green, blue, gray, and white, and have never been varnished. They are in an excellent state of preservation, only a few minor restorations having been necessary, such as a few touches on the border and the sails of the ships.

117, 118, 119. PANELS IN THE FIRST AND SECOND PARLORS OF THE ALSOP HOUSE

THE ALSOP HOUSE[1]

THE unique frescoes in this house stand apart from the others. This is due to their superior execution, classical inspiration, fine rich color, and the excellent drawing and decorative quality that mark the end of our historic fresco period.

They are distinctly Pompeian in style, but as a whole are more subdued than those of the Buried City. Gods, goddesses, dancing-girls, and cupids, with the usual classical accompaniment of birds and flowers, are seen everywhere, but always placed with a certain restraint.

The delicate designs show an astonishing fidelity to nature even to the most minute details; this is especially true of the morning-room, where the birds, insects, plants, and flowers seem to be actually alive.

The house was built in 1838-1839 by Richard Alsop, who died before it was finished. His widow, who completed it, was a French woman, and naturally was influenced in its furnishing and decoration by the prevalent Empire style created from the frescoes of Pompeii by Percier and Fontaine.

The walls were not decorated until after the installation of the furniture, as evidenced by the fact that the wall behind the large mirrors at opposite ends of the double parlors was not painted.

These frescoes were unrivaled by any in the country at that time except those in the National Capitol, which were executed by the Italian artist, Constantino Brumidi, between 1855 and 1880. The resemblance between the two groups in style, subjects, and decorative quality is so obvious that it is quite possible that they were executed by the same hand.

Brumidi, who painted several frescoes in the Vatican under Gregory XVI, came to America in 1849, when the French occupied Rome. He lived three years in New York, executing a number of mural paintings in churches. In 1852 he decorated churches in

[1] Photographs by courtesy of John de Koven Alsop.

Philadelphia, and went to the City of Mexico, where he remained until 1855. If the rooms in the Alsop house are his work, they were painted between 1849 and 1852.

The Alsop house is a large two-story structure, with walls covered with a light pinkish brown roughcast.

114. FRESCO OF ERATO IN THE FAÇADE OF THE ALSOP HOUSE, MIDDLETOWN, CONNECTICUT

The nearly flat roof with wide projecting eaves, the wings and piers, give it some resemblance to an Italian villa, in perfect accord with the frescoes within.

A unique feature of the façade consists of three white classic female figures, each one painted within an arched panel representing a niche. Between the two central windows in one of these panels (50 inches wide and correspondingly high) stands a figure of Erato with her lyre (fig. 114), painted to represent a white marble statue having drapery shading to a brownish tone in the shadows with a gray background arched at the top. On the left wing is a smaller figure which resembles Juno beneath a large urn, while on the right wing (fig. 115) stands a figure of Victory, with a wreath in her right hand, also beneath an urn. Just under the eaves there is a wide frieze, covered with scroll figures in shades of brown on a cream background.

The entrance is through a small vestibule on the right. At the foot of the wall opposite the doorway, painted to represent an open marble colonnade with clinging vines through which can be seen sky and clouds, stands a pictured red flower pot with a plant.

From the vestibule the hall extends through the center of the house and to the upper story and is lighted by a glass dome in the roof. The walls, pinkish cream and gray in tone, are lined off like stonework with large panels and a festooned frieze in sections.

This treatment extends into the upper hall, the staircase wall having gray and white female figures about six feet high in painted niches, as on the façade, one of which is an exact copy, on a large scale, of one of Canova's famous dancing girls.

Over the figures extends an elaborate scroll frieze in gray and white.

From the hall open the double parlors, separated by a wide arch; the dining-room, originally only half its present size, its frescoed medallions of fruit and flowers now covered with wall paper; and a small but charming room whose walls are painted to represent open arches through which can be seen sky and clouds, with birds and flowers.

The unusually beautiful colors in which all these rooms revel have the soft, velvety, rich effect characteristic of tempera, and their restraint in tone and mass is a pleasing surprise.

On the écru background in the double parlors, between the tall French windows opposite the chimney-piece in each room, are large panels, two to each room, on each of which is a classic figure about twenty-one inches high, within a circle of gold beads.

In the first parlor (fig. 116) appears a dancing girl holding a golden cup, the clear, rich, flesh tones shading to pink. She is clad in a red tunic, with a skirt of greenish gray, and waves a blue scarf. The panels are outlined with stripes and a thin red line, and in this room have corner-pieces of a deep blue shade. The room is finished with a frieze composed of a Greek fret in gray and white tones.

The right panel in this room (fig. 117) has a figure of Flora clad in a saffron tunic and greenish skirt, holding aloft a bunch of flowers. The smaller spaces of the walls and over the

115. FRESCOES OF THE URN AND OF VICTORY IN THE ALSOP HOUSE

doors are filled with panels on which are clear-cut scroll figures with birds of a pale golden brown. On the chimney-breast (fig. 120) stand two cupids lightly poised one on each side of a greenish tripod or altar which has a golden base and top, from which issue red flames.

To the rear of the altar stand crossed shepherds' crooks, and beneath hangs a festoon of flowers in natural colors.

116. PANEL OF DANCING GIRL IN FIRST PARLOR OF
THE ALSOP HOUSE

The center of the ceiling is covered with an elaborate design within a double square representing perhaps Phœbus, clad in a red robe, standing in a chariot drawn by red and white horses racing through the heavens. Beyond this centerpiece are semicircular festoons of flowers with birds and butterflies, with corner-pieces of winged victories in flowing draperies of red, blue, or white, the whole enclosed by scroll figures on which at intervals are placed rosettes of carved and gilded wood. The T-shaped corner-pieces are deep blue in color, the vine yellowish in tone; the festooned flowers are a medley of yellow, white, blue, red, and green.

120, 121. OVER-MANTEL FRESCOES IN THE FIRST AND SECOND
PARLORS OF THE ALSOP HOUSE

The second parlor is similar in design (fig. 118), one panel having a figure in blue with white skirt and red girdle, who is playing on golden cymbals.

On the other panel (fig. 119) another dancing figure, remarkable for delicate flesh tones, in pink drapery with a golden girdle, is playing a triangle as she dances. The stripes and cornerpieces in this room, while having the same pattern as in the other, are painted a pale golden brown.

The chimney-breast (fig. 121) also has two graceful cupids in brilliant colors, with blond hair and bluish white wings, placed on either side of another green altar. Its base is worthy of more than a casual glance, as it is an unusually fine scroll figure which has bright, rich tones almost iridescent, for they shade from red to orange-yellow, through buff to pale green, with a charm of color harmonies seldom seen. From the base hangs a festooned vine of pale green. There are also a gray moth and a fly, done with great skill. On the ceiling of this room is another heroic subject (fig. 122), Jove with his thunderbolts riding through the heavens on a golden chariot drawn by black eagles. All around him are dark clouds. In the corners are winged victories, while on each side of the double square central figures are two festoons of flowers, with butterflies and blue birds.

The small morning-room vividly reminds one of those rooms in Pompeii on whose walls are painted landscapes or distant views, as if one were looking through open

122. CEILING OF THE SECOND PARLOR OF THE ALSOP HOUSE

windows or arcades. It is always bright, a perpetual garden with its birds and flowers, regardless of the changing northern seasons.

The walls are painted to represent open arcades with wicker work rising from a base of interlacing hoops of a brown color, through which can be seen the distant sky.

Over the trellis (fig. 123) grow dark green vines excellently drawn and colored, enlivened with brilliant flowers, pink or violet, with a red tiger lily in their midst. A

126. OVER-MANTEL PANEL IN THE MORNING-ROOM OF THE
ALSOP HOUSE

123. PANEL IN THE MORNING-ROOM OF THE ALSOP HOUSE

large green macaw with red head and wings and yellow neck balances himself upon a hoop, while just below a black and golden butterfly flutters, and above is a large brown one bordered with black. On each side of the window at the end of the room (fig. 124) are more very natural green vines with bunches of red and white grapes, morning glories, and an oriole in brilliant black and red. Then more red and white flowers and shady green vines (fig. 125), a yellow butterfly, more birds, red and gray, violet grapes partly hidden among the leaves, a Louisiana tanager, black and gold, red head, and yellow breast; then a black beetle amid delicate pink flowers.

124. FRESCOES IN THE MORNING-ROOM OF THE ALSOP HOUSE

On the chimney-breast (fig. 126) on a cream background outlined in brown and red is the only figure which in any way corresponds with those in the other rooms,—a woman bearing aloft a burning torch, her brilliant flesh tones in strong contrast to her green draperies. Around the room extends a dado outlined in white and lavender.

The ceiling has a square centerpiece (fig. 127) outlined in brown with red corners. It is composed of flowers,—red, lavender, white, and green,—with a narrow panel of filigree, while at each end are larger panels representing lattices and vines through which the sky is seen, with small grayish brown sparrows whose heads are tilted forward in a very inquisitive manner.

These frescoes were painted on the plaster with tempera, the side walls being also treated with a preparation which preserved the paint to such an extent that the wall paper, which for many years covered the frescoes, was taken off without injury to them and also allowed the accumulated dust and smoke to be removed.

125. FLORAL PANEL IN THE MORNING-ROOM OF THE
ALSOP HOUSE

The ceilings were not so protected, but they were never covered with paper. While cleaning the walls of the second parlor a black spot was seen beneath the cupids, but when an attempt was made to remove it, it was found to be a fly carefully drawn and colored.

The birds are marvels of detail, being exact copies from the colored drawings in Wilson's *Ornithology,* the first authoritative book on the subject of American birds.

127. CEILING OF THE MORNING-ROOM IN THE ALSOP
HOUSE